CW00870753

All rights

This revised edition published in 2013 by

My Life My Africa Book

PO Box 1543
Randpark Ridge
Johannesburg
2156

ISBN 978-1481181129

Edited by Cheryl Ramurath

Cover Design by Joanne Theron and
Debbie Snoek

Cover Photography by Kim Page

This book is dedicated to the One who placed the Voice within me and called me to follow it's lead. But then I cannot ignore Dad, who gave me wings to fly; Mum, who has been my first call whenever I needed anything, and who has never let me down; and Tibor … my favourite brother … how many times have you saved my worthless butt!

a word from the author

I am no literary scholar or expert in any field. I am, at most, a human being who is navigating his way through this human experience; asking questions and stumbling after answers.

This book is *my* story, based on *my* experiences, and so it is filled with *my* opinions, thoughts and philosophies. Some of these have remained with me and some have changed over the years. I write everything simply as a way to express the truth of my life as I have journeyed along my Path, and I am well aware that I am not qualified, nor do I desire, to be the person who makes such bold statements about anything, as if I know some absolute truth that no one else does.

Please forgive the lack of photographs. I chose to not take a camera, because I felt that it would create a barrier between me and the people. Although I am sad to not have the pictures, I cannot measure the value of the experience, so it was worth the sacrifice.

Please also forgive my language, if it offends you in certain places. Truthfully, as much as I would like you to believe that I am perfect, I am not. My poop smells and I do use 'foul' language, a lot of which flows out my mouth when I am in severely stressful situations. All through my travels, I have kept a journal, and this has been a place for me to write freely and without judgment. In these journals, I have screamed, cried and cursed a lot, as I have stumbled along my Path, in search of Love, Freedom and True Community. Throughout this book, you will see *italicised* sections, and these are actual extracts from my journals. In the interest of truth, I have chosen to print these without editing, so that you get a glimpse of my Soul. No pretence. So I am sorry if it offends you, since this is not my intention, however, I make no apology for who I am, the emotions I have felt, and the way that I have expressed them. **If you believe that the spiritual man should hide his weaknesses to project an image of perfection to the public, rather than be transparent … now is a good time to return this book and get your money back, or else you will be offended.** Respectfully, I thank you.

Please also note that I am South African, and this book is written in South African English, so there might be spelling, grammar and colloquialisms that you are not familiar with. I have chosen to not adapt this to another form of English because I wish to remain true to who I am, and where I come from.

And lastly, if you are trying to Google certain people or places, please note that I have changed *some* of these, to protect identities.

My intention in writing this book has been simply to share my story, as a piece of the greater story, in which we all play an equal part. My hope is that you and many others would be inspired to see the beauty of your own story, and to share that with the world, so that we can all learn from each other, break down these horrible walls of fearful separation that we've constructed, and grow together in loving unity.

Thank you for sharing this Journey with me.

Please, enjoy the ride.

The value of life lies not in the length of days, but in the use we make of them; a man may live long yet live very little.

- Michel Eyquem de Montaigne

0

Reawakening

I didn't expect to see my Dad standing over me when I opened my eyes. I didn't even know that I was unconscious. But none of that mattered as I reached for the pocket on the right leg of my cargo trousers, because as soon as I had my hands on the dollars, I knew that everything would be alright.

But my pocket was empty.

I looked up at my Dad with a slight sense of confusion, knowing that a simple phone call to The Lobengula would clarify everything, but again my pocket was empty – no cell phone where there should have been.

My eyes went back to my Dad and, as he saw the urgent pleading in them, he gently responded.

"Lie still boy, something bad has happened."

I heard him and already had a feeling that things

were not quite the way they should be, but I don't think I 'got it'. So I looked at him for a while until I felt compelled to shift my gaze and scan my surroundings for answers.

Above me, I saw a damp-stained ceiling and around me were glossy white walls riddled with paint bubbles.

I turned my head to its side and saw a contraption of metal tubes primitively welded together, providing support for an inch-thick foam mattress covered in hospital-style white plastic. And when I turned my head further to see the black-and-white checked floor that supported us all, I felt a dull pain at the back of my skull.

It is only when I reached for the pain and returned a hand stained with blood that I grasped how 'something bad' had indeed happened.

That was November 2005.

If there is a God, he is within. You don't ask God to give you things; you depend on God for your inner theme.

- Bruce Lee

1

The Call

Five years earlier.

In the same way we *just know* when the phone is about to ring, or when we meet a person and we *just know* that we will be friends for a long time – I *just knew* that the voice behind Real Africa was one I could trust.

Like two stars gently coming into sight as the day loses its light, two words switched on within me.

Real Africa.

They carried no instruction and I felt no emotion attached to them, they simply appeared, flickered and gained steadily in intensity until I could no longer ignore them.

And like a boy cannot resist the urge to follow the first firefly his eyes ever land on – desperately curious to discover where it goes – I *just knew* that I was about to embark on the journey of a lifetime...

*****

My mid-life crisis came early; I was only 23 when I awoke to the realisation that my life was a pretence. Doing well at university on a path that promised much success, after decades of sacrifice made by my parents that I could neither comprehend nor appreciate, I decided to drop out.

It wasn't an easy decision, and it was even harder to act on, because it affected more people than just myself. But two years of restlessness, frustration, sleepless nights, countless questions and a whirlpool of emotions led me to a place that demanded a decision. I needed to take ownership of my life, to make a choice and to follow it, regardless of the consequences.

All I needed was to find the balls to voice that decision to my Dad and the thought of *that* tortured me, because in my heart I knew that I would never be free unless I went with his blessing. If he refused, I would have had my freedom stripped away, forcing me to remain in a life that brought me nothing but bitterness.

It was a nerve-wracking idea and I decided to take him out for a round of golf to ease my own anxieties. I guess I also comforted myself in the knowledge that screaming and shouting was something completely forbidden on the golf course, so it seemed like the ideal setting for me to break such disastrous news to a man who had sacrificed his life for my education and well-being. But I did it and am deeply grateful for having the Dad I have, who gave my simple and childlike heart a chance.

I remember the day well. It was a good round of golf we were having, where Dad was two shots up as we went into the back nine. My version of the story says that the stress of what was inside me was the cause of a few irregularities that gave him that early lead. But then on the 14th hole, on the fairway down to the green, I began to pour out my heart. The next four holes were the quietest moments I have ever experienced on the golf course and, I don't know whether it was my relaxed state of mind after shedding my burdens or whether it was Dad's broken state of mind after taking them onto his shoulders that caused it, but I ended up winning that round by a stroke.

"Boy, I have never told you what to do," he said

after two weeks of silence at home. "You are your own person and I love you for that. I know you have not conjured up this idea overnight, but have put deep thought into it. I have always told you that if you can dream it, you can be it; and if you believe it, you will achieve it, so if this is your Path to follow, then I won't stop you. Just promise me that if I let you do this, I will see that smile on your face again."

If there was a bluff, my Dad would have exposed it in that moment. But there was none.

I had spent my whole life pretending, trying to be what everyone else wanted me to be, trying to 'keep the peace', trying to 'fit in',

I had done it all, everything I was told to, and I was tired of it. There was no bluff.

Of course, there was the obvious question about why I would not complete my degree first, to keep as a backup if all else failed. My honest response to that was that if I carried a safety net, it would be too easy to rely on during my toughest trials, and that would defeat the purpose of what I was trying to achieve.

This prompted the next challenging question that came from my mother.

"What exactly are you trying to achieve?"

It took a while for me to find the answer to that, but when I did, it set me free. The truth is that all I was trying to do was discover my own potential. And I figured that I would never truly know that until I placed myself in situations that stretched me beyond my perceived limitations, in situations that left me no choice but to face my deepest fears and to find a way through them. If I carried any backup, it would have been too easy for my fear to win and keep me stagnant.

My heart painted a smile across my face and in an unseen realm, the Path I was birthed to walk began unfolding ahead of me in ways I could not have ever imagined.

I went back to Cape Town, withdrew from university and stood like an infant in front of my new life. I felt excited, naked and lost, all at the same time. Life was mine to live, or mine to lose, and there was nobody besides myself who could ever claim responsibility or whom I could ever blame.

Not knowing where I was going or how to get there made each day a terrifying prospect. How 'today' began depended largely on the outcome of 'yesterday', and 'tomorrow' was a mystery until 'today' reached its end and revealed my next step. The result was a constant feeling that I had no control on either the direction or the outcome of my days and it was both frightening and purifying.

For every day that I walked into the unknown, I began experiencing parts of myself I had never tapped into before, characteristics I was born with that had lain hidden from the world under piles of fear and lies for years. Abilities, passions, laughter and desires were all given opportunity to reveal themselves as soon as I stepped outside the restraints of convention; the moment I stepped off everyone else's projected path for my life and stood alone in the wilderness – *my* wilderness – then my fears, doubts, secrets, loves, lies, strengths and affections all came to light.

It was magical.

People actually noticed and commented on how much brighter and alive I looked and this encouraged me to probe deeper into my new discoveries. As I did, my Path opened up and a new pattern emerged. Where my conditioned-mind had once controlled the direction of my days, a silent voice within me – who I know as spirit – slowly enforced itself as my new leader. But there were practicalities I needed to face, because Dad made it very clear that for me to walk my own Path meant that he would stop supplying my pocket money. And that was quite an issue, because I never truly grasped how much support I had received throughout my life until it was taken away.

I took to the streets in search of work, boldly approaching every restaurant I could find. Whether it was as a bartender or waiter, I was confident that – after my gap year on kibbutz in Israel, and as a cocktail barman in London in '94 – my skill to serve people would help earn me a decent living. But my childish confidence quickly dwindled as each day brought me home as equally jobless as I had begun. The trouble was that it was winter, a time when the restaurant trade is noticeably low for the Mother City. My initial zeal for my new Path quickly eroded together with the last bit of my bank account as each day passed fruitlessly by and month-end approached demanding a rental payment. However, as my will weakened and resolve crumbled; as my plans fell to dust and my self-reliance failed, something mysterious sprung up.

It was an ordinary weekday when my group of mates went out to mingle with the world. There was nothing memorable about the evening – just a bunch of youngsters sitting around a table, drinking beer while surreptitiously searching the room for attractive girls we'd be too shy to approach. But at some stage someone mentioned Café Bardeli.

I don't remember why or what other information was attached to it.

I don't remember who said it or why I noticed it.

I just remember the words.

Café Bardeli.

That night as I lay my drunken head on the pillow, it was Café Bardeli that whispered me to sleep, and when I woke the following morning to walk the streets of Cape Town in search of employment, it was Café Bardeli that walked with me.

A few weeks later, completely unrelated to anything I've just recounted, my housemates and I decided to watch a movie at The Labia, a cinema with a reputation for topical and non-conventional movies, and the cinema that introduced me to Caligula.

By the time evening came for our movie, I was at the end of another unsuccessful day of job-hunting and deep in a state of self-doubt as I pondered the possibility that perhaps I had made a mistake in choosing this new life; that perhaps it was some giant hoax of the universe and that I was at the butt-end of a bad joke. And because of my absent state of mind, I drove right past the cinema.

Realising my error at the intersection, I decided to turn left and double back.

It was just after dusk, when the sun seems eager to sleep and moves quickly out of sight, that I stopped at the junction with Kloof Street. As I stared blankly at the traffic light – almost willing it to turn green – in the top left corner of my vision, a neon sign flicked on.

Café Bardeli.

From that moment forward it felt as though I was being carried along the crest of a wave – fully aware, yet not in control. The traffic light turned green, I crossed over the road, parked right below the sign, climbed the stairs and walked straight into the coffee shop.

"Welcome to Bardeli! Table for one?"

I was greeted by a short, plump, warm and infectiously friendly girl named Carla, with dark hair, heavy makeup around her eyes, and chewed fingernails.

"No, thank you. I'm actually looking for work."

As I opened my mouth to speak, my whole story – from the time I dropped out of university until the neon light sign switched on – came tumbling out. In a weirdly inexplicable way, I felt as if Carla was actually waiting for me and that our meeting was a pre-arranged appointment.

"That's cool." she said. "We actually need more hands on the floor. Grab a seat at the bar, have some coffee and I'll call Andrew."

I was enjoying both my coffee and the vibe of the place when the owner came and seated himself beside me. It was an informal affair – again feeling as if it had all been staged and that we were long-time friends – and when my coffee finished, our conversation ended and I left.

I was late for the movie and never made it to the Labia that night, but I was intentionally early the next morning for my new job.

Café Bardeli. It was more than a job. It was the light on my understanding that I am more than the sum of my thoughts, five senses, and all the information I have been selectively fed throughout my life. It was the beginning of my realisation that somewhere within a hidden and sacred space a greater force is at work – a force connecting me to a bigger story in which I am not alone.

Cape Town back at the turn of the century felt like a re-enactment of what I saw in movies about the '60s and '70s. We were all on a spiritual quest – tired of the conventional way handed down to us and exhausted with a self-indulgent and materialistic world devoted to accumulation and consumption.

The city was full of restaurants, bars and clubs, and our underground zeitgeist moved amongst these.

We were young and free spirits with malleable and wide-open hearts, but such freedom came with vulnerable ignorance and inevitably – over time – we all stumbled into the same ditch as our predecessors of the Beatles' generation.

We knew what we did not want. That was clearly defined for us by the establishments, institutions, governments and other such worldly systems. We had no trouble identifying the enemy and being *anti* it. Our trouble was that we could not clearly define our destination. We had an ideal, a vision, a hope for a future where Love ruled; where all people lived together in harmony, and loving relationship without boundaries was the goal of humanity. But there was no clear path to follow. It's not that we were blazing a new trail, because we weren't. It's just that in all the generations that had gone before us, nobody seemed to have left a manual-for-life for us. We all knew what we were running from, but none of us were clear on where we were headed, and that led to a slipway I didn't see coming.

October to March is *big season* for the hospitality industry in Cape Town, and anyone working the night shifts as a waiter in the right venue counted on pocketing around R800 (eight hundred South African rands) untaxed cash each evening. Five shifts per week – you do the math. It was money for nothing. I'd finish work around midnight with a pocket full of cash and then head off to a local pub to socialise with other like-minded people who were asking the same questions as me.

White, black, fat, bald, straight, gay, gothic, tattooed, clever, insecure, cocky, creative, architect, surfer, bookworm, unsuccessful entrepreneur, married, single, pregnant, analytical and downright dull – we were a diverse group of people just trying to be human with each other.

And it was good.

There was no person, cultural norm or societal standard standing above us; no self-glorifying leader who claimed authority. We were just human beings seeking and sharing together, gently revealing truths about ourselves and learning how to live with them in a co-inhabited world. And the conversations that flowed were entertaining, if nothing else.

"Love – it's not so much about trying to define it. That's pointless – kinda like trying to describe 'blue'. It is what it is and you either like it or you don't."

"Exactly. And we wouldn't all be here if we didn't want Love."

"Exactly. So we need to change our approach."

"Huh? To what?"

"Where? Where is the source? There must be a spring that Love bubbles from. Surely it's that source we want to find and connect with?"

"I hear what you're saying, but that's some dangerous shit, bru. The next thing you know we're all gonna be dressed in suits and singing hallelujah or strapping dynamite to our chests and running kamikaze down the highway."

Laughter and another round of drinks.

"Yeah, we seem to be backtracking towards religion here. Isn't that what they do – hold up some philosophy, proclaim it as the source and then feed you with enough fear and insecurity for you to follow blindly?"

"...and bring your tithes and offerings … bring all your money, in the name of god, or live with guilt for the rest of your life!"

"Dude, seriously, have you taken your tranquiliser today?"

"If Love is what we hope for, then surely we must be able to each approach Love in our own way and with our own language, because I don't want to compromise any part of my identity just to connect with Love. If that's the case, then it's just more bullshit I don't need."

"Trudat. Love is Love – unchangeable, all-embracing. And because of that nature, Love surely shapes itself to meet each of us where we are. We don't need to change – Love does it on our behalf so we can remain true to who we are."

"So then … there is only one Love but many ways to connect with it ...?"

"Just as there are countless people with unique traits, so there must surely be countless paths leading to the Love that created us all."

"...and therefore, many different expressions flowing outward from the same Love. Brilliant ... are you going to light up that *reefa* (also known as toke, ganja, spliff, mahanga janga, mary jane, herb, zol, bud and a host of other names), bru or just keep it in your pocket?"

This is what you would have walked in on if you had seen me out and come over to greet, back in the days of Y2K. These dialogues and my endless contemplations over them, matching them against the works and lives of some of – who I consider to be – humankind's greatest thinkers are what gently tugged at my own thinking. (Bob Marley, Jesus Christ, Gautama Buddha, the dude who wrote the Bhagavad Gita, Socrates, Plato, Paulo Coelho, and Krishnamurti are a few of these)

As our awakening unfolded, we began to witness the struggle between our inherited worldviews and our heart's desires. We acknowledged – within ourselves – how revolutionary changes were needed in our own thinking for us to progress.

19

And as we considered the options to smash our mind-sets – to start afresh in our intellection – we stumbled upon the *love drug*.

I can't imagine how much ecstasy was consumed in Cape Town back in those days. We were all on it.

There was not a night of the week short of a party – DJs were mixing some of the funkiest tunes around, and we were all high and on the dance floors. With the love drug there was no need for us to consciously alter our thinking – to search our minds for destructive patterns and then try undo them; all walls were stripped down as soon as the drug kicked in. That was the beauty of it – on ecstasy there were no boundaries and no conflict – the mind was a super-absorbent sponge, accepting all things without prejudice.

And where prejudice and judgement are absent, fear and doubt are impotent.

It was beautiful to dance in a crowd with nothing but confidence; to experiment with the rhythm of our bodies – unafraid to make mistakes and grow from them; to meet a stranger and dive instantly into a depth of conversation that would ordinarily take years to discover if we ever managed to put aside our insecurities.

It was worth it.

Now allow me to be very clear at this point. I am not a supporter of the drug industry and I do not recommend drug usage for anyone. In fact, I strongly warn against it. However, though I am most thankful that I managed to get out before being destroyed by it all, I am also deeply grateful for the part it played in my awakening.

We travelled fast as we claimed new ground, but it came at a cost – it was all drug-induced. What started as a passionate search for Love became a yearning for an emotional experience that could not be found outside of the drug-high.

I was a better dancer … when I was high.

My relationships were deeper … when I was high.

Friends were plentiful … when I was high.

My philosophy was bulletproof … when I was high.

My belief was rock-solid … when I was high.

And Cheech and Chong (either you know them or you don't) were the funniest dudes on the planet ... when I was high.

And when I wasn't, Love became a distant illusion and I became a stranger to myself. What started as the search of a free spirit became the cycle of a slave caught in a dream so detached from reality that the only way to keep it close – to keep it 'real' – was to get high.

In April 2000, the cry of my Soul became so deafening that I could no longer ignore it. There was a great Love drawing me into a relationship that would surpass all others – I had tasted it back at Café Bardeli. Unfortunately, I had allowed myself to disconnect and get caught up with impostors, and could feel myself dying inside. Being one of those kids who never gets anything done unless he takes a radical decision, I took a week's break from work, detoxed, and climbed up Table Mountain with fierce determination.

Dear God. I don't know who you are. I don't know whose interpretation of you is more correct. I don't know whether I'm supposed to say 'amen' at the end of a prayer, or whether

Jesus is actually anything more than one culture's attempt to control the world through fear-induced religion. I don't know if there's anything like heaven or hell, or whether I'll burn in a fiery furnace for liking the Buddha, the Baghvad Gita, mahanga janga and Bob Marley. I don't know about any of this and – quite frankly – I don't care. So I'm not talking to the god of these things. Not talking to the god of human understanding and interpretation. All I care about is Love. Without Love, everything else is meaningless. So, God of Love – if you exist – I am talking to you…

I was at the top of the mountain and had found a rocky ledge away from all the hustle and bustle of tourists. It was quiet up there – I could literally hear the breeze. The climb up had tired me out, and my exhaustion together with the surrounding stillness and inner turmoil led me to a place of brokenness with no façade, no pretence and no attempts to please, satisfy or convince others. In that moment of honest shedding, the totality of my life came into vision.

My years of compromise, deception, loneliness

23

and rejection.

The strain of my will-power driving me in an unwanted direction.

My free-spirit year of drugs, alcohol and the illusion of Love in fleeting friendships.

The impact of all these slammed into my consciousness like a grand piano off the seventh floor onto a pavement outside a bookstore. And in the debris it left behind, I awoke.

I was alone up there, unbeknown to anyone. I was a university dropout without any degree or diploma. I had no girlfriend, lover, Soul-mate or companion to share the fullness of my life with. Neither did I have the courage to even begin a relationship. I was reliant on mind-altering substances for my 'happiness'. I was a mess, really, offering nothing good to the world, and giving my parents no reason to feel proud.

My Soul raged.

I hate this world! I hate the judgment and segregation of it all. I hate how we all establish our own empires to divide us from each other. I fucking hate the religious systems that

24

support and promote one race, one class, one culture as superior to another. I hate that innocent people must suffer in poverty; that children die from hunger and cold while others complain about their under-floor heating that's not working properly, or the sirloin that wasn't cooked to their satisfaction at the last restaurant they visited, or the service of the air hostess on their last flight to Thailand, or the filter coffee that wasn't hot enough at their last church service. I fucking hate it all! And if this is your world, if this is what pleases you, then I don't want it.

Each word came hurtling out of me with such force that I was left breathless. And in that empty space, the penny of my own understanding dropped into my consciousness.

I am not willing to live any longer in a loveless world. We're all slaves here. We're all paralysed with fear and self-doubt. We're all so emotionally insecure that we spend our life's energy trying to win the approval of others – the way we talk, the way we dress, the gossip we engage in, the people and philosophies we follow, the products we buy. We measure ourselves by the colour of the bank card we pull out our wallets, and value ourselves by how much stuff we accumulate, but nobody cares about anyone else. We're selfish haters of the world and all who occupy it. Surely this cannot be. Surely, Love, if you are real then this hurts you more than it hurts me. Surely, Love, if you are as powerful as I hope you are, then you have a way to overcome this. Surely, Love, you are not standing by helplessly as your instruments rebel. I believe in you, Love. I believe you have a way to heal all things, to return the balance. I'm sorry for my selfishness, my self-indulgence. I'm sorry for my egotistic ways. I'm sorry for all the pain I have brought into this world, for the lives I have hurt, neglected and ignored. I'm sorry for making myself more important than others, more important than you. I'm sorry, Love. Forgive me please. Give me a word and I will listen. Give me a direction, and I will walk. Call me and I will follow.

My childish rant shifted towards a more sincere confession, and in that tilt I stumbled upon the Unyielding Warrior within me.

Love, if you do not exist then I do not care to exist. What's the point? And if you are just some bullshit that is only found in Hollywood movies, then I'm not interested. I'm equally unhappy if your greatest display is only found in fleeting emotions and romantic fairy tales. I don't care for religion or academic debates, and scientific proof is a waste of time that only reduces the limitless to the simplicity of our human minds. If Love is not the greatest force in the universe that has created and which sustains all things, then what am I living for? And if Love is not something within me that I can tap into, be empowered by and receive guidance from, so that I become an active partner in the great redemption plan for humanity, where all things on Earth are restored to perfection, then why exactly is it worth my time to stay alive? No, I would rather sit here and slowly waste away than continue living with such emptiness.

I am just not willing any longer...

Who am I? Why am I here? Where am I going? What's my purpose? Where is my joy? How do I find it?

Talk to me, please.

That period of waiting was the most purifying moment of my life. I have never known such helplessness. To use some casino talk – I had cashed in all my chips to play on a single bet. I kept nothing up my sleeve, no insurance, no Plan B. I had written off every other way of life as meaningless and fleeting, and had resolved on that day that it would be Life or Death – Love would call out to rescue me or I was going to die on that mountain without saying goodbye to Mum and Dad.

Nobody was around to watch, no-one to hear my cry, this was deeply personal.

The sun travelled its usual course, but the day felt much longer as I was made to revisit every voice of fear, doubt, mediocrity and compromise that had ever tormented me during my life. Looking back, I guess that battle was needed;

that it was necessary for me to face my demons in a moment of intimacy before embracing a way diametrically opposed to everything I had ever been conditioned with.

My shadow stretched slowly down the mountainside and guys who had been playing some touch-rugby on one of the university fields below brought their game to an end as light snuck off the field. And somewhere in that moment, I heard something from a place within me that I had been unaware of my whole life.

Real Africa.

Intrigued and feeling safe, I decided to probe the mysterious Voice.

"What do you want me to do with Real Africa? Is that your word? Is that your call? What am I supposed to do with that?"

Go where I say and write your story for the world to read.

And then there was silence.

That was April 2000.

For the next two years, I could not shake the

Voice from my consciousness, yet I could not get any further instruction either. It was two years of torture, intrigue, frustration, excitement and insanity all rolled into one.

The kind of stuff that, when you're in it, you know you're alive.

February 2002, on my way to Johannesburg to visit my parents for a holiday, I was at Cape Town International Airport when the Voice I had first discovered within me spoke from outside of me to reveal the vast extent of its capability and reach.

I was browsing around Exclusive Books, trying to find wisdom in the spirituality section when I heard my name being called.

"This is an urgent call for Passenger Naidu, please report for boarding immediately."

I made my way out the shop past the till, greeting the cashier as I did so. I smiled, and as she turned her head to return my greeting I caught a glimpse of a glossy blue magazine cover behind her left ear. On the bottom right hand corner – in bold yellow print – were the words "**Real Africa**".

Without hesitation I bought the magazine, boarded

the plane and turned to the article with two years' worth of bubbling expectation.

The main article was four pages long and focused entirely on the nation of Zambia. And in every paragraph, on every page, the words "**Real Africa**" were written in bold and jumping out at me.

It was all I needed.

In that moment the two-year wait was worth every second. And perhaps if it were not for the wait, I would not have been prepared to handle the call.

I don't know.

As it turned out, however, when I reached home, I began immediately packing for my trip.

Mum was the first to notice that something was up.

"What are you doing, boy?"

"I'm going to Zambia." I childishly smiled in return.

"Are you mad!" It wasn't a question, but she quickly followed it with one. "And why on earth are you going to Zambia?"

"Because God told me to." I smiled again, knowing full well that – being a good Christian – she wouldn't dare argue with God.

"Mad child." She uttered as she left the room.

I was young and naïve, but behind my words was a sincerity that Mum knew too well. There was no stopping me.

Perhaps Mum's right. Maybe I am mad. Maybe I'm not. But how will I ever know unless I follow what I believe, to discover its truth?

Real Africa … Game on.

Only those who will risk going too far can possibly find out how far one can go.

- TS Elliot

2

Stepping Out

I hoisted my backpack over my right shoulder and walked out my parent's home to the parked car where Mum and Dad waited, deep traces of concern etched across their faces. I loaded my pack into the trunk, slammed it shut and turned to face them both. All the words that needed to be said had been spoken in the weeks leading up to that day, so the only thing left to do was take the parting photographs, which remained stuck to the door of Mum's fridge for the next five years. As soon as that was done, Dad and I were pulling out the driveway with Mum's forlorn figure standing behind us, wondering if she'll ever see her youngest child again.

I felt like an alien as we entered Park Station. There weren't many brown or white people like I was used to having around me, and that 'first-world' shopping-mall vibe that I had grown so comfortable with throughout my life was noticeably absent. We walked through the station to the shabby-looking bus that was assigned to my departure and stood next to it in silence.

It wasn't long before I realised that I needed my father to leave; I needed to be alone to process things in my head and Dad knew that too, so we both moved in for a farewell hug. It was difficult to let go, and I lingered in the safety of his embrace for longer than a 'brave warrior' should. But eventually my brain reminded me that my decision had been made and that leaving was inevitable, so in one fluid motion I withdrew, said goodbye, tossed my backpack into the cargo-hold and boarded.

I was early and there were many empty seats, so I made my way to the back and sat down, deep in thought.

Ahead of me lay a journey northward along an unfamiliar path to the South African border, across the Limpopo River and into Zimbabwe. From there I expected to travel through the night in a volatile and violent country amidst its 2002 elections – a period that left approximately six million people in need of food aid. And if all went well and without incident, I was supposed to arrive sometime the following morning in Zambia – a destination I believed I was called to reach.

What the fuck! What am I doing? This is crazy! Where am I going?
Why didn't I buy a traveller's guide or something?
Why couldn't I have carried just one safety net?!
This is stupid. I'm feeling a lot of anxiety right now.
Where am I going to sleep?
What am I going to eat?
I don't know anyone there. How am I gonna find my way around?
Will they even accept traveller's cheques? Do they even have banks?

Am I doing the right thing?
Am I making a mistake?

Fuck it, how will I know unless I try?
What if I back out now and lose a great opportunity?

When will this damn bus start moving?

(during my Journey, I have kept a journal.

Sometimes I would write in it as things were happening. Other times I would reflect, whilst on a bus or a up a tree. Whenever you see *italicised* sections, these are actual extracts from my journal. And in the interest of truth, these are unedited)

Choosing to walk an untrodden path in pursuit of Love, guided by the voice of my heart was a beautifully romantic idea until the Journey actually started and I was faced with the uncertainty of it all.

Was I going to a place with cities or was it all rural African mud huts?
Would I find electricity and running water?
Was it a peaceful place like I hoped for, or was it full of violence and corruption, like Zimbabwe?

The truth is that I had moved on a whim and was both clueless and unprepared.

What I did have though, was my trusted 25-litre backpack, a 15-year-old Swiss army knife, seven pens, 576 empty pages to journal my story in, thirteen thousand rand's worth of traveller's cheques and a childlike belief in an unseen Voice only I could hear. I opened my journal and began reading, as a way to encourage myself.

"True beauty is terror. When we find ourselves in front of something truly beautiful, then we are filled with terror; but if we are strong enough in our Souls, we can rip away the veil and stare at the naked, terrible beauty in the face; let God consume us, devour us, unstring our bones and then spit us out … reborn."

I found these words in a book called *The Secret History* (written by Donna Tart). I can't remember much about the book, but somehow these words etched themselves on my heart and remained there for many years as I waded through the battlefield of life. They helped me be courageous in times of fear, brave in times of uncertainty and childishly foolhardy in times of extreme trial and temptation. I was deeply focused on their wisdom, trying to encourage myself that I was doing the right thing when Robert, a tall, dark Ugandan man approached and sat himself silently beside me. I barely had a chance to notice or offer the man a greeting, because as he arrived our bus began to move, and my Journey into the unknown took on a new twist.

What I expected to take 24 hours was about to take much longer.

Our bus was a simple one with no on-board videos or music, no air-conditioning or toilet. The result was that we made several stops along the way to allow for passengers – male and female, young and elderly – to head for the bushes.

Now the idea of men jumping off a bus, 'whipping it out' and peeing freely on the side of the road is something as normal to me as mutton curry. But to see elderly – and I'm talking beyond the age of fifty – women getting off the bus with napkins in their hands to climb up the roadside embankment and go behind some shrub to pee, was something I was not quite prepared for. But it happened so often that it eventually became normal to me.

Seven hours into the trip we came to a halt just south of the natural dividing line between South Africa and Zimbabwe – the Limpopo River.

A lone filling station stood to our left, stranded in a sea of dusty rock.

Primitive shacks constructed from waste pieces of metal, cardboard and wood – all hammered together with a bucket-load of nails – lined the road on our right, in single-file. On the ground in front of them, oranges, tomatoes, potatoes, boiled eggs, spinach leaves and live chickens were displayed for sale.

Our bus passed by and entered through a boom-gate into a wide parking lot outside a face-brick building with an administrative feel to it. We all disembarked, stepped through a plastic tray, stood on a wet blanket – apparently to counter the spread of livestock disease – and walked toward the sign that read 'Immigration'.

About 20 metres from the entrance to the office, we reached the back of the queue of people who had jumped off the other five buses travelling the same route as us. As I waited patiently, I began to understand why our bus driver had driven at such breakneck speed: every driver raced each other to beat that queue. In fact, a bus company earned its reputation as 'good' or 'bad', based upon this ability alone.

I stood for about an hour under hostile African

sunshine before the fat, colourfully dressed African mamma in front of me finished her business with the immigration officer. I stepped forward and handed over my passport. The seated officer – drenched in sweat, with a face towel clutched in one hand to periodically dab his forehead – took the document and threw a searching glance at me. He then turned his head and began exchanging words with his fellow workers in a language I could not understand. Any previously invisible signs of uncertainty began to express themselves across my face when the man looked up at me, smirked and shook his head.

"Where are your stamps?"

"What stamps?" I asked.

"Your exit stamps!" The fat, black man questioned me in a threatening tone of authority, and in an accent similar to what you would expect to hear in a movie portraying African terrorists.

"All my stamps are there," I responded, visibly shaken.

"You are not South African. You are illegal, maybe Pakistan."

And with that, my passport slipped under the officer's mouse-pad and panic began ringing within my fragile mind as I noticed wry smiles on the faces of the other men behind the counter.

"We will detain you. Come this side, get out of the way the bus must go. You will sleep in the cells until you speak the truth!"

I was a raw blend of confusion, loss and hopelessness, and pleaded with many heartfelt sentences all beginning with "my brother", but none of them had the desired effect. A dark and real fear began squeezing me as irritation bubbled up amongst my fellow passengers who stood behind me in that long and frustrating queue, and my energy quickly faded away.

Our bus had departed at nine that morning and by the time I was being questioned and delaying the further progress of our trip, it was already getting dark. The immigration office became noisy, all of it in languages completely foreign to me, and I still remember that nauseous feeling as my spirit weakened. After a solid hour of public humiliation, the gods of travelling humour chuckled themselves complete and sent the bus-driver to my rescue.

He exchanged just a few words with the officer, who duly stamped my passport and released me together with the rest of the passengers to cross over the Beit bridge on foot.

Holy crap! I have not even left my own country yet and this shit has already started. These are my own people … fellow citizens … what's going to happen when I cross over to Zimbabwe's side? Sweet Jesus, please don't let me get raped in a prison cell.

I walked slowly and contemplatively across the bridge.

I knew a Zimbabwean once, he approached me at an intersection in Johannesburg around ten one night during a particularly cold winter in which evening temperatures dipped regularly below zero. He wore a T-shirt and a torn pair of jeans, and carried a pizza box in his hands. I don't usually entertain beggars, but the guy stood so humbly and patiently at my window that I eventually relented.

"Please sir, I am not begging from you. Some white guys have given me this pizza and I just want to go back to my bush so I can sleep."

It was too difficult to refuse a man such a request, considering how my conscience reminded me of my bed at home being heated by an electric blanket.

"What's your name, my brother?" I asked.

"Chabalali, sir," he replied in a gentle tone.

I chatted with Chabalali-the-Zimbabwean for the duration of the five-kilometre trip to the nearby parking lot of a shopping mall, where I was guided to an unobtrusive bush which he described as "my place".

Chabalali had an older sister and a younger brother back in Zimbabwe. Their parents died at an early age and, as long as he could remember, it was his sister who had taken care of them. Eventually when they could no longer handle Zimbabwe's oppressive regime and the poverty and hunger it brought to them, they decided to head south toward greener pastures.

South Africa was their Promised Land and they journeyed on foot to the Limpopo River, which was their final hurdle before true 'freedom'. Chabalali and his siblings walked without hesitation into the river, their eyes focused on South Africa, but that focus was disturbed when the first crocodile took away his sister from right in front of his eyes.

Chabalali – determined to reach dry land – instinctively stepped in front of his younger brother to protect him. They either needed to turn around and get back to Zimbabwe, or continue their journey to South Africa. Whichever choice they made, the crocodiles were not going away. They knew this when they started. Chabalali kept walking, talking continuously to his little brother to encourage him and help keep his mind focused. But then came a rush of water and a scream.

Chabalali did not look back.

He knew what he'd see.

His brother was gone.

When he reached land he was a shaken cocktail of emotion. He had made it. He was in South Africa. Freedom was his. But as he cast his eyes behind him to see a river tainted red by the blood of his last family members, he felt the pain of the price that was paid.

"Chabalali," I asked, "do you not regret coming to South Africa?"

"No sir," he replied, "life is better here."

I left the young man at his bush, where he curled up into a ball with a bottle of wine and some leftover pizza.

"Please sir. Don't think bad of me. This wine is the only thing that helps me sleep."

Chabalali's Zimbabwe, a country he felt was worse to live in as a free citizen than an alien immigrant on the streets of South Africa, was the same Zimbabwe I walked towards as I crossed the massive steel suspension bridge.

After my shenanigans at South Africa's border, I was eager to pass through the Zimbabwean immigration process swiftly, but my anxiety followed me as I joined the rest of my fellow travellers to patiently endure a further two-hour delay. Five immigration officers stood behind the counter littered with posters of Robert Mugabe, but each of them seemed intent on finishing their coffee and conversation before attending to us.

And not one of us said a word.

About 200 adult men and women remained silent and still, jammed into a sweat-inducing simple brick-and-wood structure, as if we were naughty children in the headmaster's office.

I felt frustrated because my tired body desperately needed a rest, confused because I was still uncertain of the trip that lay ahead through the night, and scared because I was in a foreign country where anything could happen to me and – since my cell phone signal had officially died – could call nobody for help.

Thankfully there were no irregularities and, eventually we were all cleared and tiredly made our way out and back onto our bus.

Robert-the-Ugandan was first to speak.

"What happened back there?" he questioned in his rich, baritone voice.

"The guy didn't believe I was South African. He said I was illegal! And he said there were stamps missing in my passport, but they're all here," I replied. I had not spoken for about three hours and my words came rushing out. "He said he wanted to lock me up. I didn't know what he was talking about. And he wouldn't give me my passport either; he just kept it under his mouse-pad. He even made me speak Afrikaans to prove I was South African and even after I did this he still didn't believe me."

Robert calmly listened until I was finished, and then he spoke.

"It's what they do. They can see when somebody is new to road travel and they use this scare tactic to force a bribe out of you. When I started moving across borders five years back, I was also a victim. I have paid many dollars in my time. How much did they get?"

"I didn't pay anything! I didn't understand what was going on."

He smiled.

"Next time, travel with a sports magazine and keep ten dollars in it. When you find yourself in such a situation again, simply smile and ask the officer if he watched the weekend's football games and when he looks at you, hand him the magazine to review the score. Your passport will be stamped and the trip will continue without any delay"

Robert smiled again.

With the outside temperature dropping, the windows misted up with the breath of 80 passengers; the air hung heavy with the stench of armpits, sweaty feet and un-bathed bodies, and Robert-the-Ugandan just closed his eyes and drifted off to sleep.

It was nine pm.

The bus set off into Zimbabwe and I sat quietly in my seat, unable to sleep, read, think or cry. I had just undergone emotional stress more intense than anything I had previously experienced in my 24 earthly years, and I was only 12 hours into my Journey. Fear sparked a torrential flow of very searching questions within me, which I restlessly pondered as the bus rolled onward.

Around midnight, a critical diesel-shortage in Zimbabwe forced us off our route to search for fuel in the most unlikely places. And while navigating through rural gravel roads littered with scrap metal, broken bottles, iron sheeting and nails, we punctured a tyre. Half of the passengers instinctively set off into the night while I and the others remained to offload the luggage and assist with the tyre changing.

The combination of my recent border experience, the stench of the cabin which I had grown accustomed to, and the old grannies climbing the banks to pee behind bushes had removed me so far from the life I knew that I simply followed without a question. Five hours later, as the morning light began to cast her net across the land, the guys who had disappeared the night before began arriving with huge plastic containers on their shoulders. I woke from my semi-sleep on the roadside, covered in dust and mosquito bites, eager to see what was happening. Words started being exchanged from a distance and while the men walked with the containers, the bus drivers began fiddling around the fuel tank. I quickly summed up that the hunt for fuel was successful and that in the containers was the diesel we needed to cover the remaining few thousand kilometres of our trip. I then began to wonder whether the fuel was found at a registered diesel vendor, but quickly stopped myself. The containers were emptied, the bus's tank was filled and our journey continued – a full

12 hours behind schedule – towards the Chirundu border-post on the northern side of the Zambezi River.

The sun was still rising as our time in Zimbabwe reached its end. We were on a narrow dust-road, and a simple wire gate ahead of us was the only indication that it was time to stop. Everyone slowly woke up, stretched, yawned some foul-smelling breath and stepped off the bus with me close behind, and when I saw them dry-brushing their teeth with their fingers, I did likewise. Except they weren't actually dry-brushing, and some kind old woman who saw me looking a fool handed me some toothpaste to confirm that.

I took it thankfully and continued brushing.

When I saw everyone spit to their side, I did the same and wiped my mouth on my sleeve – a habit of mine since childhood that annoys my mother to this day, almost as much as my other one of picking meat from the pot while it is still on the stove.

I joined the line that formed next to a rusted cargo container and followed the queue into an all-steel room, one by one, to face the Zimbabwean-exit authorities.

Thankfully it was a painless and swift process, as Zimbabwe seemed happier to let us go than it was for us to enter. I exited the container and was directed by an official with a big gun to my right to cross another enormous bridge, this time over the Zambezi River – Africa's fourth largest. I looked across and saw a building similar to the administrative one at Beitbridge, placed on the right hand side of a large clearing resembling a concrete helicopter pad.

My stomach turned as I considered the possibility of more harassment.

Towards the back end of the clearing was a guarded wire gate, and the whole yard was enclosed by a cement wall. My bus drove past me and parked itself behind a queue of other buses on the left of the clearing, and my eyes were immediately drawn to the movement of people that took place between bus and building.

The path through immigration was quick and easy and I was eager to continue unhindered through to the border's exit. As I left the building, however, expecting to find my fellow travellers settling into their seats for the last leg of the trip, I found instead so much frenzied activity that I felt as though I had teleported into an Egyptian marketplace (albeit without any Egyptians). It was only then that I began to learn how the immigration process is just a tiny fragment of the Chirundu experience.

Our bus was third in a line of four, all of which towed trailers packed with luggage – with each trailer big enough to carry about two horses. When I stepped outside, I saw everything being emptied onto the ground. And I do mean everything; every bag from each cargo hold and trailer of four busses was strewn all over the concrete clearing in no apparent order.

Thinking of my lonesome backpack amongst the debris, I wanted to cry. But when I considered how little I stood to lose compared to everyone else, and how nobody else seemed at all anxious, I intentionally calmed myself to try and understand exactly what was happening.

It turned out that every bus passing through Chirundu was filled with small-time African traders who had travelled to South Africa to purchase their *katundu*. Clothing, shoes, milk, rice, toothpaste, body cream, soap, motor vehicle spare parts, computer components, CDs, spices, cell phones and accessories, corn cereal and anything else you can think of was sourced in South Africa, transported back to Zambia and sold for profit.

All of these items and any other luggage is known as *katundu*, although I later learned that on the streets there was another slang use for it to refer to testicles. For example: "Hey man, your *katundu* is showing. Pack it away."

As I asked questions, I found out that most of what was sold in Zambia was bought in South Africa – unless it was imported *fong kong* goods (Chinese imports) that came in through Tanzania, or the locally produced *mvubwe*, a powder consisting of a variety of crushed roots, leaves and god-knows-what-else which gives a man a slow, steady and strong erection for an enjoyably prolonged period, with none of the Viagra-aching after effects (so I've been told … on both accounts).

Fifty-litre plastic containers, massive suitcases and industrial-strength polyester bags were all offloaded by one team of luggage boys while a second team waited on the ground to grab and roughly stack them onto massive trolleys before wheeling them off.

The luggage boys were very grubby youngsters in their late teens and early twenties, beaded with sweat, dressed in sleeveless vests, and wearing trousers that were once long but had since been cut below the knee with something I could only guess was a blunt knife or sharpened spoon. These boys were dirty, smelly, rude and crude, but played an essential role that kept Chirundu alive.

The place was shambolic.

Passengers shouted to boys who climbed into trailers, offloaded *katundu* and packed their trolleys before melting into the crowd.

Officials walked around in their westernised uniforms, engaging freely in conversation with many people, maintaining their sense of authority yet bending freely to the breeze of easy conversation.

Hands met, shook and held onto each other.

Magazines and newspapers exchanged.

Cool drinks and cigarettes went back and forth.

And everything happened amidst the perpetual rumbling of a gentle laughter I have since grown accustomed to.

At least 300 people moved around in a small space patrolled by a goofy-looking man in green camouflage with a semi-automatic gun slung over his right shoulder. I tried to find my place but could not make sense of anything – where to stand, sit or walk, or what was happening to the luggage being shuffled around on trolleys – so I decided to remain still and that paid off. Eventually I ended up in a queue that moved me slowly to the exit gate, where I was warmly greeted by a fat and jovial woman who cleared me to leave the fenced area of customs and immigration, to enter the country of Zambia.

Concrete turned to dust and the setting changed.

A boy came up to me with a cardboard box of dry-ice containing just a few bottled waters.

A woman smiled at me with her offering of dried fish displayed on a little piece of lost concrete at her naked feet.

Another woman walked around with a reed bowl filled with groundnuts.

Two boys stood side-by-side in a stall as big as a dwarf's phone booth crudely constructed from idle pieces of wood.

Another two leaned against a nearby wall continuously counting out various currencies in their possession, as travellers haggled and bargained with them.

And the local rastaman sat alone in his makeshift shelter with some sweet reggae music keeping the peace while he sold airtime, sweets and single cigarettes.

Two hours passed by quickly and I was yanked from my new world and its many attractions when I noticed our bus starting up and edging forward without warning.

The marketplace was thrown into a frenzy.

Men ran, women swore and cursed, children tried to sell their last sweets and cool drinks, foreign exchange deals quickly ended, luggage boys were yelled at, and bags were thrown through windows into open compartments or handed to complete strangers. Some people were rushed out while others swarmed in and, through it all, the only thing I was certain of was that the bus never stopped moving, so I grabbed my backpack and instinctively pushed forward until both my feet were on-board.

Five hours later we arrived in Lusaka, the capital city of Zambia.

At the time I was convinced I had lived through a miracle to survive such a hellacious trip, but years later I came to realise that I had simply experienced a normal day in Africa and that the saying, "Africa is not for pussies" is one that carries some weight.

The assault on my westernised world view continued as I got off the bus. Zambian people are not pushy and intrusive – like the folk I found in Morocco or Egypt, for instance – but the situation in which they lived, and their strategies to survive nudged my thinking into new directions.

A barefoot young girl held a tray of boiled eggs

in one hand as the other balanced a baby on her hip.

An elderly woman gently thrust an orange in my direction, competing for my attention with a younger girl who balanced a plastic tub on her head, filled with corn fritters.

And then there were the others who offered me stalks of sugar cane, blank CDs, sunglasses, bananas, bottled water, canned cool drinks and US dollars.

But the one who caught my full attention was the man who shoved his keys right against my chest.

"Taxi … taxi…?"

I began to realise I was in a semi-developed area when I heard his call and saw the dangling keys in front of me.

Okay, so I take a taxi and then what? Where do I tell him to take me? Where the fuck am I going? And what, do I just arrive and immediately start marketing myself as a clueless stranger? I think not.

I shrugged off the many attempts made by taxi

drivers and street traders to earn their day's wage from me, walked over to the pavement, threw down my backpack and sat on top of it, waiting for my next step to reveal itself.

When you have come to the edge of all light that you know and are about to drop off into the darkness of the unknown, faith is knowing one of two things will happen: there will be something solid to stand on or you will be taught to fly.

- Patrick Overton

3

Finding Faith

The heat was dry and intense.

My naked arms felt like pieces of Kingklip under a searing grill. But I found an odd sense of freedom in my helplessness as I sat alone by the roadside.

All around me the city moved and shifted as I have come to expect cities to do, but there was a different pace and feel to it – relatively slower than what I was used to and strangely peaceful.

I found nothing impressive about Lusaka.

The tallest building in sight was about ten floors high and towered above everything. Most of the other shops were two-storey buildings selling nothing out of the ordinary – takeaways, clothes, electronic goods, furniture and the like.

It was a busy space, though.

Traffic moved in both directions along a road that ran straight down the middle of where I was, which felt like a little town similar to Howick.

The road itself was divided by an island of worn-out grass and small trees resembling a Third World nation's attempt to appear westernised, and I noticed many cars – mainly white and baby-blue Toyota Corollas – that filled the roads and parking spaces on either side.

Then there were the people; crowds of them on foot, walking around and talking to each other, either face-to-face or on their cell phones.

And once again I noticed a lot of laughter and smiling.

I've never seen anything like this. These people all look genuinely happy. That's weird. And they're walking around but they don't seem to be rushing, which is something I'm not quite used to either.

Okay, what do I do now? Just sit, I guess. And wait. Surely if I wait long enough then something will come along to move me?

I wonder where I'll sleep tonight. I don't see any banks. I only have traveller's cheques, I wonder how much I'm going to lose on commission...

There must be a better way to do this. I can't just sit here. What are my options?

Money is only going to get me so far and then it will run out. And I don't think looking like a beggar is going to work ... it might get me some sympathy and a few coins, but that's about it. Fuck man, think!

A lot of time passed by, which gave me ample opportunity to think. And it was a challenging process. I tried to think of everything I had ever been taught at school and university; I thought about the many things I had learned through the various avenues of information that I had been exposed to and conditioned with by the society I had grown up in; and each time I did, I grew more helpless at how ill-equipped I was for the life I had chosen. And maybe that was the point, because the more helpless I felt, the deeper my desire for a friend became, until I realised that I was at a fork in the road. I could either look at every person around me as a stranger, or I could choose to see them all as my friends.

A smile gently creaked through my stubborn face. And it wasn't the smile-at-the-camera or it's-nice-to-meet-you smile, but more like the baby-looking-into-the-eyes-of-its-mother-coz-it-knows-that-its-very-existence-depends-on-this-woman smile.

It was a mysterious moment that radically impacted my perspective on life. And as I awakened to the beauty in each face that walked past me, I finally accepted how my Journey depended mostly on my relationships with those around me, and very little on my schooling, culture or financial status.

"Where to?"

No introduction, no greeting, no pleasantries. Joseph was a total stranger walking along the pavement, going about his daily business, when he saw my smile and felt compelled to return it and approach me.

"I'm not quite sure," I replied uncertainly, challenged by his approach. "I was hoping to find a backpackers, but the people I asked on the bus did not know what I was talking about."

"Backpackers? I also do not know this thing. Where from?"

Some of my initial fears subsided as I relaxed in his use of the English language.

"South Africa." I answered.

"Aaah, South. And you are on a trip?"

"Well, in my spirit I heard a Voice call me to Real Africa. I have followed that call and now I am here, but I don't know where to go next."

Talking with Joseph returned the same feeling I had experienced with Carla-the-waitress back at Café Bardeli a few years earlier. My heart, mind and spirit seemed to all click into place, and a peaceful confidence came over me.

"Why did you not greet me or introduce yourself?" I questioned. "Where I am from, people always greet first."

"And in the culture where you come from, do people ever stop to engage with you and ask the pressing question you need to help you along your way?"

"No, I guess they don't."

"I believe the place you're trying to reach is The Valley. Come."

Joseph called out in a foreign language to a couple of guys standing around some Toyotas, the biggest of them – wearing a black tank-top – smiled, shouted something back and began walking over to us. We met half way; he took my pack from me, threw it in the boot of his car and opened the back door. Without thinking, I jumped in and we drove off.

We left the city and drove about 20 minutes before entering a sparsely populated area with a few simple buildings and a lot of shacks. The feeling was kind of a ghetto/township vibe I wasn't entirely comfortable with. As I looked with judgement on the community we were in, we turned up a poorly lit road and stopped.

"This is my house." Joseph smiled at me, "and that is a guest lodge where you can stay. Come and meet my friend, he is the manager."

Joseph paid the driver, took my luggage from the boot and led me towards the guest lodge. It was not what I expected. 'Guest lodge' to me meant a place above my income bracket where tourists with dollars, pounds and euros stayed. But in Zambia it meant nothing more than a place for guests to lodge, and had more of a hostel feel than anything else. A pretty young lady greeted me as we entered, exchanged a few words with Joseph and then directed me to my room.

Holy fuck, what a shithole! But that's okay, I guess, because it has got to be ridiculously cheap ... and cheap is my friend, so I think this will work out just fine.

The bed was a single, thin foam mattress on a metal frame. Beside it stood a small, wooden bedside table just big enough to hold a Gideon's *Bible*, a jug of water and an empty glass.

A mosquito net hung from the ceiling with so many holes, and mosquitoes trapped inside that it seemed safer to sleep on the floor.

There was an en-suite bathroom, but not like you're thinking. The floor was covered with what looked like black-and-white plastic wallpaper. The bath tub was dotted with brown stains where cigarettes had been left to burn out. The toilet had a black seat that was leaning up – broken – against the wall, and though the place had running water, it only flowed from the cold tap.

I threw my pack on the bed, disturbed the mosquitoes and walked out to find my friend, curious about where my Path was carrying me.

As I came down the passage, I saw Joseph talking with another man who was smiling together with him and nodding in exuberant agreement. I saw a lot of that since Chirundu; everyone seemed to know each other well, and conversations were highly animated, filled with smiles, holding-of-hands, head-nodding and so much laughter. As soon as they noticed me, I was invited to join them at the bar, which was really a courtyard that looked like something I could have thatched while drunk, using some wild grass from the side of the road.

There was a simple wooden counter on the left, hammered together with some nails and a few pieces of scrap wood. Behind the counter was a chest freezer filled with the local beer – *Mosi*. The name is taken from one of Southern Africa's natural beauties, the mighty *Mosi oa Tunya* – the 'Smoke that Thunders'. But you probably know it as 'victoria falls', a name that makes me really angry because the falls do not belong to Victoria and it was not the English who discovered it (this is why i haven't capitalised it). I mean, how would you feel if I walked into your house, rearranged everything in your kitchen cupboards and re-named your child, just because I felt that your home did not suit my culture?

I'm just saying.

The barman, who was the manager and also Joseph's friend, handed me a Mosi with a smile and invited me to sit on one of his rickety chairs made from wood and tied together with bark. I obliged, settled back and let the Mosi flow.

Both Joseph and his friend were fascinated by my story, and they fired a ton of questions as they sought to understand both me and the Voice I claimed to follow.

"You don't know anyone here? And you have never visited Zambia before? Are you not scared?"

[unspoken answer: No. No. I'm shitting myself, but I don't show it.]

"And how long will you stay?"

[unspoken answer: Haven't got a clue.]

"What about your family, do you not miss them? How will they know where you are? Do you call them? Can they reach you? Do you have a cell phone?"

[unspoken answer: I do. They won't. No. No. No.]

"Is this bag of yours the only *katundu* you are carrying? And you will manage to live with just this for your whole trip?"

[unspoken answer: Yes. I hope so.]

"And this book, what is it about? Have you written one before? How long does it take to write? Will we be in it?"

[unspoken answer: Not entirely sure yet. No. No idea. Hmmmm ... didn't think of that.]

Laughter. More Mosi.

"This is a wonderful thing, you are very brave. I will be most happy when your book is complete."

The Mosi was at work in my bloodstream, my nerves were calm, my tongue had loosened, and I was feeling the need to be honest.

"So will I," I said, "It all feels so impossible right now. I started with absolute faith that I will find my way as I move along, but the challenges I have faced are more than what I expected. I feel like I am walking blind … and I am only at the very beginning."

"You see, in Africa we believe in Spirit," Joseph began, and he had a look in his eyes that forced me to pay attention. "And it sounds to me like this Voice you speak of is the voice of the Spirit in you. So if Spirit is the one who has called you, and Spirit is the one you are following, then Spirit is the one who is writing the book. There is nothing to worry about, you only need to be patient to allow time to do its work.

"You will find many people along the Way who will be there to help you and like I have already said, do not worry. Just remember, every man reaches his destination if he continues walking. So you will also reach yours, if you just keep walking."

"This is Lee." Joseph continued to beam at me, finally introducing the man who we had been sharing company with since we arrived. "He is my good friend and will call a taxi for you tomorrow to take you wherever you need. He will also help you with your question of this thing you call 'backpackers'. As for me, it is time to go home to my wife."

Feeling quite emotional, I gave Joseph a mighty man-hug.

"Thank you my friend. I was just a stranger sitting on the side of the road, completely lost. I don't know where I would have been by now if you did not come to talk with me. Thank you. You have earned your place in the book." I smiled.

"Do not worry," Joseph assured me, "in Zambia, you are free."

And he sealed that promise with the same warm smile he approached me with, when we first met earlier in the day. I hugged my friend again, shook Lee's hand and walked to my room with a new-found freedom to settle down for a night's rest and some scribbling in my journal:

Everything that's going on is just so foreign to me, it's blowing my mind. There's no way I could've prepared for this. I mean, I knew this was not gonna be like Israel, England or Europe, and I expected it to be tough. I also know that the first few weeks are the hardest to get through. I know this shit. I've done it before ... but it's just not the same. This whole place, culture and experience is totally whack! I'm in this shithole 'guest lodge' surrounded by some kind of squatter camp or something and there's music blaring from all around. It's a Wednesday night, the Zambos are having themselves a royal shindig, and I feel like I'm in the middle of a night club!

I have no plan. I really don't, and that scares the crap outta me. No plan, no guide, no contacts... All I got is faith... or delusional hope in some invisible Voice inside me ... what if I'm wrong ... maybe all the mahanga janga has finally tripped a switch in my brain. I don't know. This place is not geared for backpackers at all either, and that's like the only security blanket I was counting on. I feel really small, weak and helpless.

Oh well. What am I gonna do besides continue?

I can't believe this Joseph guy though. What a godsend. I swear I was totally lost until he came along. And that smile! Man, I have never seen anything like it. How weird that something so simple has made me feel so safe. Just imagine, the last thing I saw for the day was a smile, and the last words I heard were 'In Zambia, you are free'.

That's cool.

The following morning, as I stumbled around the guest lodge in search of something to eat, I found a taxi driver at the reception desk waiting to take me to *Cha Cha Cha's*, which, I discovered, is the perfect backpackers for anyone landing in Lusaka for the first time.

I was lazing around the pool when I first saw Benson and Chibichabo (they both introduced themselves with their English name. When I asked for their real names, Chibichabo told me his, but Benson did not have one. That really pissed me off, kinda like victoria falls). They walked into the yard as if they were at home, and that drew my attention straight away.

Cha Cha Cha's was on a quiet road in a residential area, surrounded by a high brick wall with barbed-wire running along the top. When I arrived the day before, I was required to show my passport to the gatekeeper for him to confirm with the bookings sheet before I was let in. I hadn't booked and was made to face a series of questions before eventually entering. Benson and Chibichabo, however, walked straight in without any questions. Intrigued, I approached them with a Mosi each – a habit I decided to wholeheartedly adopt from Joseph and Lee – and we spent the rest of the evening sharing stories and becoming friends. I learned that both of them had completed their schooling the previous year only to discover that, due to poverty, there were no options for further education. Then they researched the job market and found that there wasn't really one, so they finally befriended Wade, the owner of Cha Cha Cha's, and started up a Township Tours service for backpackers. Eager to know more about the heart of the land and people, I arranged a no-cost tour with my two friends for the following day.

It must be the Indian in me, but sometimes I am able to negotiate a deal that will leave a person naked, yet thanking me for my generosity.

I was awake and waiting when my friends arrived.

It was a quick and uncomplicated affair; they walked into the yard, saw me and greeted. I walked over to them, out the gate and into the waiting taxi, which drove off as if he already knew where we were going. It didn't take more than 10 minutes and we arrived.

Good God! Soweto Market. I've never seen anything like it!

Of the one million Lusaka residents, about 100 000 of them shopped at Soweto Market, which has absolutely no relation to the Soweto in South Africa (in case you're wondering). The chaotic setting, cacophony of sound and rancid smell that all violated my westernised mind-set was the heart of what I sought to break my preconditioned thinking and nudge it into new territory.

Spanning the space of approximately two soccer fields in haphazard arrangement, the Soweto Market was completely informal. It was the market for the people, by the people, and has its own unwritten rules that all people – even the police – subscribed to. Everyone who flocked to the big city for their fortunes and failed, made their best effort at Soweto to trade in *salaula* (unwanted clothing from the West that is shipped into Africa in bales) stay alive. I can't give you the exact figures, but I did learn that the *salaula* trade comprises a large and significant chunk of Zambia's economy.

The place smelled alive.

Groups of men stood around fires that burned in drums and discarded truck tyre rims, which boys tended to as they roasted small cuts of meat. The men picked from the fire as they drank their beers, talking and laughing amongst themselves.

I looked around and saw hundreds of people, maybe thousands, all talking and laughing.

I struggled to find space to move. People were all around and up against me, and I felt like a dry leaf being tossed around in a breeze, completely not in control of where I would end up.

My nose picked up that familiar and sweet scent of mahanga janga in the air, competing with the smell of dust, stale beer, sweating bodies, roasting meat, burning fires, and something sour that I could not identify.

And Bob Marley, local Zambian music and some Congolese Rhumba provided the backing track as we continued our walk.

My eyes searched curiously.

The ground we walked on was a field of dust littered with empty bottles, paper, cardboard, groundnut shells and sugar cane pulp.

There were also no real buildings to speak of.

A teenager in a wooden stall with a hair shaving machine and a bottle of methylated spirits was a barbershop.

Wooden poles holding up a sagging roof made of tent canvas. Two simple wooden tables covered with a cheap plastic table cloth decorated with drawings of oranges and watermelons; a jug of water in the middle. People sitting around and eating with their hands and even picking from each other's plates – that was a restaurant.

A lady seated on a stool. Two women behind her talking to each other as they braided her hair, with a young girl holding an umbrella to provide shade was a hair salon.

And shebeens were everywhere (illicit taverns selling alcohol and tobacco. In South Africa, these are legal. In Zambia, they are illegally legal, similar to marijuana in many countries, and sell alcohol that is mostly smuggled from Mozambique and Zimbabwe). Some, simple brick and plaster structures big enough to hold 20 to 30 people. Others, more temporary wooden structures like the restaurants. The music I heard came mostly from these establishments, through very distorted speakers. I looked inside and saw men – young and old – seated on upside-down beer crates, drinking, talking and laughing.

So much laughter that it was impossible to ignore.

And then there were other trading stalls set up on the naked earth, packed next to each other like tin cans in a grocery store. Meat, toiletries, vegetables, tobacco, hair products, *mankwala* (traditional medicine made from herbs, roots, bark, leaves and other natural sources), bicycle repairs, motor car spare parts, small hardware and plumbing materials, and plenty of salaula and shoes – all of these were displayed on newspaper, cardboard or plastic sheets that rested on the dusty ground and served the purpose of a shop's display counter.

Pretty much everything that is shipped into Africa through the ports of Dar es Salaam and Beira was found at the Soweto Market, where the poor appeared to rip each other off by selling things they had little need for, but which a consumption-driven world had convinced them was absolutely necessary, regardless of how they could barely afford two healthy meals per day for their family. Like creams with peroxide in them, for example. I kid you not. Women used these creams on their faces to lighten their complexion because it is widely believed that beauty and prosperity are directly related to a lighter skin tone.

I say no more.

This is incredible! A whole new world. This is real – real people, real struggles, real laughter, real LIFE. No bullshit, no pretence – I'm so in love. I can feel it in my heart. I belong here. I really, really BELONG here. Back home people would laugh at the audacity of someone calling their business a restaurant or hair salon that looked like these. But it works over here. Nobody seems to care about image – a restaurant is where people sit and eat a meal; a hair salon is where a woman gets her hair done – so what if it doesn't look like the movies or magazines! And it's so weird; I have never heard so much laughter and seen so many smiles! But these are the people we usually refer to as "those poor people"? We usually look at them with pity, but they look happier than most that I've ever seen, caught up in debt, in the capitalist world. There's freedom here ... real freedom. Man I have so much to learn! I need to strip away my western mind-set, I need to just let go and fall into this experience. I need to get high!

"What are they drinking?" I asked with eagerness as I observed the jovial faces in the shebeens, and recognised that unidentifiable sour smell again.

"This is *Chibuku*. It is original Zambian beer. You want to taste?"

What a question.

Chibuku is brewed traditionally by the Ngoni people, tribal cousins of South Africa's Zulus. Also known as *Utshwala*, it is made from fermented maize and satisfies thirst, hunger and any desire to get wasted.

For the people in Zambia, I learned in my later years that Chibuku was the answer to everything – breakfast, lunch, supper and a way to forget their troubles – and at five p*in* per mug, it was very affordable.

The Zambian currency is the *kwacha* and *ngwe*, although nobody talks about the ngwe because there's really nothing to say about it.

One '*pin*' is 1000 kwacha. Five pin was about three rand, and that's what I paid for 500 ml of Chibuku.

My first cup wasn't so easy to drink. Fermented maize is a different kind of sour that takes a while to get used to, the texture is creamy-scratchy, and the thickness kept tricking me into trying to chew it every now and again. It wasn't disgusting though, so I just kept drinking until it tasted normal and, it wasn't long before normal became good.

Eventually Benson tugged at my sleeve.

"Come Philén, there is still much for us to see. We can drink later."

He was right. I hugged my new friends and danced out of the shebeen with a new resolve to eat or drink whatever was put in front of me, without question.

If the people are doing it, then I will do it. How else will I learn, how else will I make room for my mind to grow and my thinking to evolve beyond my conditioning if I do not try new things?

I needed to be careful as I continued my walk though – a ruler length from every step, neatly arranged on the dusty ground, laid a person's *katundu*. To disrupt this would be the equivalent of urinating on your neighbour's doormat – not good.

As we walked, Benson and Chibichabo educated me.

"These are groundnuts, Philén. In Zambia these are all over and we are eating them all the time, they help us with hunger and energy."

I was handed a bag of sandy pods that, when I cracked them open, held two peanut-looking fruits. I sucked the fruits out the pod and chewed them, discarding the shells thoughtlessly as I walked, and whenever a bit of sand got into my mouth, I spat on the ground. And so the procedure continued for as long as I walked, with me being just one amongst thousands of others engaged in the same act. It was an easy, tasty and fun habit.

"In Zambia we are poor, Philén. Most of the time people are surviving with only one meal in a day. A lot of that time we eat half of it and then leave the rest for when we get home because it is not good to sleep with an empty stomach – this brings bad dreams. But poverty does not earn us any rest. Life waits for nobody and we must all continue to work. But you can see Philén, this work is not like to sit in an office. This is hard work and needs much energy, more than we get from our meal. So God gives us sugar cane." (I noticed a lot of talk about God since I arrived in Zambia. Later I learned that former president, Fredrick Chiluba - in what appeared to have been a political move - declared Zambia to be a Christian nation, in 1991)

Chibichabo was right. I had noticed barefoot girls and boys within sight wherever we went, standing next to a bunch of sugar cane stalks they held upright alongside them as if they were leaning against a traffic light. Benson asked me for one pin (about one South African rand and eighty five cents), approached a girl and returned with a stalk that he broke across his knee into smaller segments before handing them to both of us.

I put the sugar cane to my mouth, savagely stripped it with my teeth, bit a healthy chunk, crudely chewed it and sucked on the juice until it was flavourless. When I was done, the pulp flew out my mouth and joined the mess of groundnut shells, sugar cane and mealie cobs that scattered the path we walked.

My Soweto Market experience reached its climax later in the day when we approached the back-end of the market under a web of electrical pylons, where the stalls and pedestrian traffic was less congested. It was also the backyard for Zambeef, Zambia's largest meat factory, where all the waste skulls of every slaughtered animal was dumped into piles that easily stacked up as high as a house. If you're trying to wrap your head around that – picture your living room, multiply its area by two and then fill it up with cow, pig and goat skulls until it bursts through your ceiling and touches against your roof tiles. That would make one of the three piles I saw in front of me.

I stopped for a moment – sugar cane in-hand – to watch a new perspective on life reveal itself.

Six men mingled, scampering up piles of skulls in search for remnants of meat.

Fat crows squawked to each other from different gathering places around the same carcasses, ready to compete.

Each time a man got close to food, he was dive-bombed by a crow, which resulted in an outburst of expletives and curses that I could only laugh at, while my grandmother probably turned in her grave. But it wasn't just me who saw the humour, because the drunken bums fell into each other's arms with hysteric laughter themselves. Eventually one of the men reached a meaty looking skull, picked it up and held it above his head for his friends to admire. I saw a scene out of an Indiana Jones movie flash in front of my eyes.

"*Mapoloyako!*" screamed another, and then they all burst into repeated hysterics.

Mapoloyako literally means "your balls", and I don't know what it is about the word, but it's been funny every time I've heard it. I dare you to shout it out as if you're insulting someone, and see if you don't, at least, smile.

Bit by bit, the six men scampered to the top of a pile, collected their skulls along the way, then rolled down to the bottom without spilling a drop of their Chibuku. When they had collected enough, they made a fire from whatever waste plastic, cardboard and rubber was around, boiled a pot of water and threw their skulls – brains and all – into it.

"They will eat this for supper," Benson informed me. "It's what they do. And tomorrow they will do the same. Sometimes when they find good ones, they sell them and use that money for Chibuku. This is how many people live in Zambia."

Loaded with Chibuku myself, and a fresh outlook on life, I headed back to Cha Cha Cha's in high spirits.

That evening in the camper's kitchen, I met Carlos-the-Brazilian-chef, a young couple from

Sweden, five German dudes and two girls from Manchester – one of whom was of Pakistani descent and had brought some spices with her. I had been craving a good curry and took full advantage of the situation as I partnered with Carlos to cook a much-anticipated meal. But it was a shocker, and if my Great-Uncle Babu was still alive he would have slapped me across my head for shaming our ancestors and the timeless tradition of excellent food that they established on this earth.

Truth is that I underestimated the ferocity of the Pakistani chilli and whatever flavour I attempted to bring out through my combination of spices and meat was lost on paralysed taste buds. But it was the perfect icebreaker for the group – we dived into whatever wine we could find, polished it all off, laughed and shared stories until the early hours of the morning.

During that time, Carlos and I connected.

"Hey. Tomorrow I'm leaving man. I'm going to Tanzania. You should come."

"Are you nuts? What do I want to go to Tanzania

for ... have you even been listening to a word I've said, I'm trying to get to The Valley, man?"

"Phil, listen here, Chipata is the last Zambian town before the Mchinji border into Malawi, man. My bus goes along this route, through Malawi and into Tanzania. You come with me and then jump at Chipata and I'm sure you can reach The Valley from there."

Carlos made some sense, although it sounded like a bit of a radical and unplanned move. But as I thought back to the day I had just experienced, I realised that there was no choice really, I was being nudged again and whether I wanted to or not, my Journey was inevitable.

"I'm in, let's go. What time are we leaving?"

"Let's leave at five. You need to be there early to get your ticket. I bought mine already, but I'm sure if we get there by 5:30am then you can still buy yours."

We looked at each other, agreed and continued drinking until our lights switched off.

I was only asleep for about two hours and was not in my best form when I felt my tent being rattled by a mad Brazilian on a mission.

"Phil! Wakey wakey man – let's go."

I heard him and I knew what I needed to do, but everything about me was slower than usual. By the time I emerged from my shelter, Carlos' tent was already down, packed and strapped to his back. And after I finished washing myself and began attending to my own tent, he was out the yard, calling a taxi.

The taxi arrived, Carlos was ready to go and I was still packing.

The frantic Brazilian screamed, threatening to leave without me if I did not hurry. I shook the cobwebs from my head, scrambled as fast as I could – continuously shouting back to Carlos to make sure he was still waiting – and finally reached the gate, but was refused exit.

My bill was settled – it was something I did at the end of each day to keep me aware of my expenses – but having decided at some drunken and early hour of the morning to travel to Chipata, I had collected no exit pass the day before, which was the only thing that would authorise the guard to open the gate for me.

From here things got a bit bumpy.

Carlos was on the other side of the fence, jumping up and down shouting panic into me.

"Phil! Come on, we gotta go, we gotta go, we gonna miss the bus!"

The security man stood in front of me trying to calm me down, but firmly refusing my exit.

The taxi driver violently abused his hooter in support of Carlos.

And then the owner's dogs – two big German Shepherds – joined the commotion.

It was a moment in need of swift thinking and a clear mind, but I lacked both and the result was painful.

My conscience was guilt-free because I knew that I'd paid and had no debt.

I also knew if I did not make the trip with Carlos, that I would lose valuable momentum, which I was something I was not prepared to do.

So in a moment of thoughtless action, I flung my

backpack over the barbed-wire fence towards the taxi's roof, which Carlos collected – mid-flight – and tossed onto the back seat.

The taxi stopped hooting and revved its engine.

With a guard to my left and two mad dogs at my heels, I scaled the fence, launched myself against the barbed-wire and tumbled to the pavement in a heap, grazed and bleeding. Without disentangling me, Carlos shoved me in the car, climbed in after and slammed the door.

Before the security man could open the gate, the taxi was off and I was headed to Chipata.

The trip should have been done in about eight hours but Carlos and I reached Chipata in six, using a bus that was well renowned for the most number of recent road deaths in the country. Hung over with a headache from hell and with scratches, bruises and bleeding holes across my body, we were thrown vigorously from side to side for the entire six hours.

As we went around every bend, *katundu* fell from the overhead compartments, crashing to the floor after bouncing off someone's head. At first, Carlos and I tried to stop them, even tried to catch and replace them, but eventually we gave up.

The bus was overloaded with people, their personal *katundu*, boxes of *salaula* and other *katundu* for sale, which all filled the passenger cabin. Most of the passengers had slept on the floor of the bus station the night before to ensure they would not miss the journey and the result was a pretty pungent smell that held us locked in.

The seats were narrow, like the ones you find in the economy-class of any cheap local airline, with three on the one side of the aisle and two on the other. Carlos and I sat on the side with three, and shared it with a fat African mamma who spilled over quite a bit onto my friend's seat. He, in turn infringed upon my space, forcing me to sit half-off the seat while balancing someone's child on my knee.

The child coughed on me.

Another one sitting on the floor in the aisle picked her nose and then continued eating her tiny packet of crisps, sucking all the MSG-loaded flavour from her orange-stained fingers.

Babies cried a lot and I couldn't blame them either.

It was very uncomfortable.

An old man snored. Two kids looked at him and giggled.

And I counted 63 heads on the 55-seater bus.

Just before lunch-hour, our bus pulled into a small town and stopped at a roadside filling station, which was two petrol pumps under a carport. We all tiredly got off the bus. Some went *'to catch a whiz'*, others went to the tuck shop to grab a cool drink, and about 10 of us stayed behind to get our luggage from below. Slowly each passenger started returning and when I saw my friend, I knew it was time. We hugged, Carlos climbed back into the bus and I was left standing alone in a foreign town, about 2000 kilometres and 3 days of travel, away from home, with my backpack slung over my shoulder. As I stood and waited, Joseph's words from a few days earlier skipped across my mind.

"Every man reaches his destination if he continues walking. So too will you reach yours, if you just keep walking."

I looked around, made a decision and started walking.

He who asks questions cannot avoid the answers.

- Old African Proverb

4

Into The Valley

Chipata town.

I was in the upper part alongside the single tarred road that ran between Lusaka and Malawi. There wasn't really much to see; a Shoprite, post-office, bank, a few filling stations, some administrative and governmental looking buildings, and the usual restaurants, bars and shebeens. I walked along, patiently waiting for my next step to reveal itself and innocently wondered about the roadside market as I tried to compare it with other parts of the world I had passed through.

For maybe 100 metres on either side, I saw a line of women with *chitenge* (colourful African material, about the size of a table cloth) wrapped around their waists. Many of them stood next to a bicycle with a big reed basket on the back, others had some *chitenge* laid out on the ground in front of them and some had their reed baskets on the naked tarmac. Whether it was in the reed baskets or on the *chitenge*, I saw a lot of daily food items for sale.

Onions, tomatoes, rape leaves, *delele* (okra), pumpkins, dried fish, groundnuts, green beans, green peppers, live chickens, eggs, fresh meat, salt, cooking oil and brinjal were all readily available for any passer-by.

I chuckled to myself.

> *I am very familiar with fast-food and take away drive-thru's – but this is like a slow-food, walk-past market. I'm not quite sure behind the reasoning of it all, but it looks like everyone buys just enough ingredients to cook a single meal. Maybe they don't have enough money to do a weekly shop ... I don't know, but there sure are a lot of people walking around, buying stuff. Why aren't they at work? Where do they get their money from? Hey, I don't know where I'll end up tonight ... maybe I should get something ... I wonder how much stuff costs?*

I spent about R5 and bought a tomato, an onion,

two brinjals, some chillies, salt and some cooking oil. I shoved them into the side pouch of my backpack and continued walking.

"Ahoy man."

It was a rasta greeting I knew well and, for me, that meant the angels were by my side and that I was exactly where I was supposed to be. I smiled and turned to meet the face behind the voice.

"Ahoy, where to?" The rastaman repeated his question.

"The Valley." I replied without hesitation.

"Come, man, I will take you."

Kayela-the-rasta touched his fist against mine and returned it to his heart in greeting, then took my backpack without question and threw it over his shoulders.

As we walked, I felt a growing discomfort with two things. I was troubled by the fact that Kayela was carrying my bag, it made me feel like a colonial exploiter. And I was also uncomfortable with the many inquiring eyes that I felt were directed towards me.

Thankfully, Kayela noticed and decided to ease my tension.

"We are used to visitors in Chipata, man" he began as we walked, "there are many people who are passing through. We see them in trucks and buses, many white people with these same bags like yours. But they all stick together and stay close to their transport; it is not usual to see someone like you walking amongst the people.

"But it is a good thing you are doing, man. To be with the people and to live like the people is a good thing, and we appreciate this. Do not worry, the people stare because they are interested and in our hearts we are very happy. Be free, man."

We walked slower than I was accustomed to, Kayela was in no rush. He greeted each person we passed by, asked after their family, about their plans for the day, and introduced me to each of them. Every time he did this, they asked about my family and the Journey I had walked that caused our paths to intersect.

Each time, I was encouraged with the sweet reminder that every man reaches his destination if he continues walking.

That short period shared with Kayela shifted something inside of me.

I have grown up in a world full of strangers whom I have been taught not to speak with. I walk with my eyes and mind firmly set on a destination and whatever people I encounter along the way are usually a hindrance, unless I can get something from them that aids me with my own agenda. I greet people with a curt hi-how-are-you-fine-thanks and then move quickly past them to continue with my day's agenda, not truly caring how they are, flirting with the superficial, but seldom venturing any deeper.

Walking with Kayela exposed to me something new. I got a glimpse of a life that is more focused on those around me than on myself, a philosophy that both deeply disturbed as much as it attracted me. And as I paid attention to this, my two guiding stars twinkled just enough for me to know that I was exactly where I was meant to be.

Real Africa.

A sudden scream jolted me from my thoughts and

back to real life.

"Kabwalala!"

I looked to my left and saw a young man backing away from an elderly and irate woman.

"KABWALALA!!"

I instinctively gravitated to the scene of the noise, with Kayela right next me, providing the explanation.

"Thief. This is not good, man."

I listened with interest.

"We do not have much money here man, so we rely on each other instead. This is good, it is the way to live, for sure. This is Africa – one love, one heart, one people, one land. But now this foolish boy wants to steal from someone. Kabwalala! If we steal from each other then we are only stealing from ourselves, and then we are dying as a people. We cannot allow this. Come, watch and you will see."

The old woman shouted again.

"Kabwalala!"

The cry was picked up by others as they heard it, and spread like wildfire. The young man who had been spotted tried to avoid the glares of the growing mass of people and slink away into the shadows, but it was a vain attempt. The crowd gathered, boxed him in and slapped him around, not violently but in a disciplining way that left him with no doubt that he'd committed a foul. He tried to resist at first, but eventually relented and was taken to the police. All the while, children looked on with keen interest. They learned as much from the drama as the thief himself: stealing is not good and has unpleasant consequences.

Kayela and I continued walking and, without warning, we approached the drop into Lower Chipata.

I imagined a meteor crashing to Earth, obliterating all life in its landing zone, reducing everything to a dusty crater that indigenous Africans later settled in and filled with stalls to serve as their marketplace.

We stood at the top looking into it, and the setting changed.

Filling stations, motor cars and buses with their honking horns, petrol fumes and disinfected buildings, tarmac, brick and roof tiles all disappeared and were replaced.

Tarred road became orange dust and the buzz of engines transformed into the chatter of people competing against the clanging of metal.

A single pathway for cars ran along our left, down into the crater, through it and up the other side and young artisans lined the left side of that. I squinted to get a closer look and saw them all hammering flat iron sheets into various shapes – bath tubs, washing tubs, *mbaula's* (fire braziers), cooking pots and other items that I could not figure out.

On the other side of the road, spreading towards and through the centre of the crater, were a host of small stalls made from spindly branches and bark, covered with bunches of wild grass for shade.

The crater was sprawling with them.

We left Upper Chipata, began our descent and, as I soaked up the sights and sounds, I smiled.

What a funny-weird experience. It's all the

same thing really, isn't it? I mean, whether we're herded like sheep from a parking lot into a sterile shopping mall, or descending into the marketplace of Lower Chipata – it's all the same thing. Some people are trading products and services, and others are buying. It's such a mind-fuck though, because I've become so used to just one way of doing it. I am so used to the shopping malls and big advertising and all that bullshit that my brain actually believes it's the only way, but then I walk through Chipata and start to see another way ... and it's refreshing. So what if economies crumble and buildings fall down, we can still do what we do ... just much simpler. Do we really need to be so scared? Are we really so dependent on the structures we've built, or have we dulled our minds to the possibilities of our human potential?

Kayela and I walked side by side as we moved closer to the centre of the crater, amongst the stalls, until our descent ended and we began the climb out the other side. He directed my eyes to a collection of white, three-ton Mitsubishi canter trucks, surrounded by waiting people at the top end of the marketplace.

"Man, we will find your transport there."

As we approached, I saw a square yard, fenced off with a low wall made from rough concrete bricks. On one side were three food outlets similar to Soweto Market, two cellular phone airtime vendors and a tuck shop that stocked cool drinks, crisps, cigarettes and sweets. There was an opening to the yard big enough for a bus to pass through, and as we entered, I saw two Canter trucks parked on the right hand side.

Kayela and I joined the group of people sitting and waiting on the wall nearby the vehicles.

The first truck's engine rumbled into action and the driver drove slowly away. I was momentarily confused about why we all remained while the truck drove off without us, but I was settling into the groove of Real Africa and began slowly trusting that all would be revealed at the correct time, if I just held my ground. So I did just that and continued spent my time chatting with the people, who were full of both questions and encouragement.

"Just remember, in Zambia you are free. Be free." I was reminded, almost as if the spirit of my friend Joseph was following me.

"And remember, do not rush. *Pangono pangono ndimtolo*. (bit by bit makes a bundle)"

The truck returned and came to a dusty halt in front of us, and what unfolded was something similar to the chaotic frenzy I had experienced at Chirundu.

The Canter was loaded full of goods; crates of beer, canned beans and pilchards, crates of cool drinks, boxes of crisps, bags of cement, drums of petrol, sacks of mealie meal, construction timber, clothes, milk, live chickens and two live goats. All these were neatly packed in the back of the truck, leaving enough room for only two people to squeeze in the front next to the driver.

At least that's what I thought.

Kayela grabbed my backpack before the truck even entered my sight and while the dust of its arrival was settling, my pack was tossed like a dead body onto the heap of other *katundu* in the back.

107

"Go now man, jump on."

Kayela spoke with no panic, but with an insistent command that moved me ahead of my own thoughts. By the time I caught up with the situation and cast my eyes around, the truck was loaded again, this time with people. Each of those thirty-something people who stood with me in that yard were also on the truck, on top of a crate, a box, a bag or someone else.

Kayela smiled at me with a look of satisfaction, as he stood on the ground and watched me depart.

"We will still meet, my friend. Kalyazi knows where to take you."

I waved goodbye and settled in for the ride.

An old woman sat at my feet next to a goat that continually fell on her as it lost its balance around each corner.

Another woman, with countless stories hidden in the shadows around her eyes, sat on the ledge of the truck opposite me, holding onto a 50 kilogram bag of mealie meal to prevent her from falling backwards.

My own left hand squeezed the neck of a pocket of potatoes to help me keep my balance. It began cramping after a while and I shifted my weight and carefully switched hands as the truck bounced and drifted across the uneven road. And as I looked around I saw that everyone was doing something similar. We were all – literally – holding on for our dear lives as the truck moved forward at startling speed.

To be honest, given our seating arrangements, five kilometres an hour was 'startling'.

Less than 10 minutes after exiting the town of Chipata, we were on a dusty, gravel road that disappeared steeply into a hazy collage of afternoon sun and wild African mountainside. A few hours later, the climb ended and we began to weave our way downward into The Valley.

I revelled in the magnificence that opened up in front of my eyes – not a building or vehicle in sight … just pure Nature.

Red earth, as far as my eyes could see, was contrasted by the rich brown and dark green of the trees that seemed to have been liberally painted across it by some great cosmic artist.

Waterholes and rivulets were randomly scattered across this scenery. Although perhaps it was not as random as I thought, because around each of these were villages of people. I let my imagination run wild, as I thought about the early days when mankind was moving freely across the land, expanding as our population increased. I thought about how groups of men would walk for miles in search of water and, when they found it, would decide to set up camp, which later developed into a settlement for their women, children and livestock.

I snapped back to reality and continued my observations.

Smoke arose from each of the villages, which comprised of a small gathering of huts, identifiable by their own uniquely earth-brown and circular walls, with bunches of wild grass laid on top to provide the roofing. And it was refreshing to see so many children walking, running, up in trees, or in the fields whacking goats and cows on the buttocks with small sticks, rather than being in shopping malls or in front of televisions, iPads and cell phones.

The scenery was breath taking in its simplicity and the harmony of life that played out in front of my eyes humbled me into silent appreciation.

I was lost in it all. Lost and in love, and I remained in that state of wonder for the rest of the journey, never taking my eyes off my surroundings; trying to soak up as much as I could for fear that it would end at some stage.

Our ride down into The Valley was done chasing after a setting sun and by the time we reached the junction, it was dark. We turned right onto a tarred road and drove for a few minutes before stopping by a roadside spaza19 shop, visible only by the candles burning inside.

A few people instinctively jumped off and began carrying away their *katundu*, while some boys emerged from behind the little *spaza* shop (an informal convenience shop, usually run from home, that supplements the income of the home owners, selling small day-to-day items) to assist. Kalyazi, the truck driver, exited the vehicle and came over to me.

"Here," he said, passing me a burning spliff. "We are in The Valley now. First we will drop off all these people and their *katundu* and then I will take you to Flatdogs. This is a good place for you to start."

It took about an hour, but eventually we turned off the tarred road, drove a bit on some gravel and then arrived at a campsite named Flatdogs. I was warmly greeted by an English woman who charged me five US dollars for the night before directing me to where I could pitch my tent.

"You can set up here and familiarise yourself. Unfortunately you're here a week before season begins, so the place is going to be real quiet. Friday night is the official opening and then you'll get a chance to meet all the owners in the area at the bar for a good party! It'll be great. Just hang in until then."

The woman walked off and I was left alone under the light of the moon.

The campsite was a large grass area that touched up against a river bank, mostly shaded by massive trees scattered around it. And it wasn't the kind of grass that you want to roll in or pitch a tent on, but rather the kind that you want to be sure you are wearing shoes to walk on. I looked around and noticed man-made ladders running up most of the trees, leading to wooden platforms amongst the branches. It made sense, so I climbed up one and pitched my tent.

In a very primitive way, my first thought after shelter was fire, then food.

I took out my gas cooker, boiled some rice, added a tomato, onion, chilli and some salt, and leaned back against a branch to enjoy an authentic bush experience as I smoked the remainder of the spliff that Kalyazi had given me.

Above me, the sky was littered with stars that I could see through the gaps in the branches of the tree I was perched in.

Around me nature moved and shifted.

A gentle breeze tickled my skin. Insects shuffled and sang.

I slowly closed my eyes and began to drift away, but then snapped awake as I became aware of nature shifting and moving below me.

I don't know what time it was, but for the hippos it was obviously feeding time. A whole group of them made their way noisily out of the river right next to me to feed on the wild grass directly below. I rolled onto my stomach to watch them through the gaps in the slats of the wooden deck that held my tent. I could hear them breath, chew, swallow and make a sound that I interpreted as a burp.

It was incredible.

From the time I first heard the Voice and made my decision to follow its call, I had struggled with constant doubt. I had enjoyed every moment of my Journey and had summoned all my courage to walk it faithfully, but there was always a nagging opponent in my mind that questioned me.

"Is this the right move? Is this the right place? Is that the right question? Are you certain that you are hearing correctly? What if you took a left instead of a right and now you think you're in the right place but you're actually lost...?"

These questions tormented me all the way, intensifying during periods of trials and challenges, constantly threatening to derail me with self-doubt. And I never truly had any answers, so I ignored them in the hope that, one day, things would become clearer. As I stared at the hippos and dozed off into a peace-filled sleep, deep within me I knew that I had arrived. I was exactly where I was supposed to be.

Friday evening came and I made my way to see what the opening of season was all about. The receptionist was right, it was a real party. I walked into the rustic little bar-area and found it packed with travellers from South Africa, Australia, Germany, Holland and the UK. The energy was electric, the music was pumping – it was any backpacker's dream start to their African tour. On any other day, on any other trip, I would have partied that night away and loved every minute of it. But for where I was in my life, I felt hugely conflicted – everything about that evening felt very un-Real Africa. The westernised music, the people, the conversations, and the MTV videos playing in the background on a television screen all felt out of place. I thought about how encouraged I was, as I surveyed the African wild on my ride into The Valley, how my heart ached to get into *that* scenery that had opened up in front of me; the scenery with huts and children and fires, goats and cows, and no electricity, radios and televisions.

Just five days earlier, I knew that I was in the right place, exactly where I was meant to be. In that moment in the bar, however, I knew without a shadow of a doubt that I was in the wrong place. Time had moved on.

My spirit sank, my breath shortened, and my anxiety increased and twisted my stomach into knots.

I turned, hurriedly walked back to the campsite, quickly took down my tent, flung my pack over my shoulders and ran for the exit.

I recognised the road as soon as I saw it – it was the one that Kalyazi had used to bring me to Flatdogs just a few days earlier. In my mind, I figured that if I ran back along that road, I would find my Path again. I was so confused by my emotions, however, that I did not stop to consider the magnitude of where I was until I bumped into something that felt like a tree trunk, but was not.

Blinded by the night, it was only when it rose into the air and trumpeted murder into the skies, that I realised I had come face to face with my first elephant. The gigantic beast returned to the ground and flapped its ears at me, all the while bellowing a deafening sound that rattled my bones.

Paralysed with fear, I crumbled to the ground and sat cross-legged exactly where I was, with my backpack still strapped to my shoulders.

I've read many books about how the universe is all connected by some cosmic energy/intelligence; how the flap of a butterfly's wings in Sudan can affect the rainfall in Shanghai; how we are all connected and coincidences are no coincidence at all but rather signposts to guide us along our Way. I've even adopted this thinking and added it to my world view; being criticised by some as an esoteric, hippie who has smoked too much of 'the good shit'. And I can't prove any of it as truth. What I do know is that as I whispered my apologies to the mighty African elephant, something happened. Was it my whisper? Was it the incredible love I have for the elephant that could be sensed apart from my words? Was it luck, God or the flapping of a butterfly's wings? I don't know, I am no authority. I just know that somewhere between her anger and frustration at my insolence, and my tears of apologetic respect and appreciation, we came to know each other. She dropped her trunk and stopped her ears, took a few paces backward and glared at me.

Her baby appeared from behind her and continued eating from a nearby tree, and the mother snorted and half turned away.

I remained seated until they were both out of sight.

It took a while to gather my thoughts and awaken to the reality of what had just happened, but eventually I did and slowly lifted myself to my feet.

Behind me was a world I had chosen to leave behind, certain that I should not go back. All around me was a wilderness covered by nightfall, filled with wildlife that could crush me in a heartbeat.

What was there to do, but continue walking?

My steps were gentler, and my pace more intentional, as I walked in pure silence, still shaken by my experience. My nerves were on edge like I have never known them to be, and my senses were acutely aware.

I heard the breeze, rustling leaves, insects, running water, footsteps and many sounds I could not identify, but which I knew belonged to the wildlife whose territory I was in.

I could smell the earth, animal dung, and the scent of a river.

And all around me, my eyes saw moving shadows.

It wasn't long before fear returned and I thought about the possibility of running into another animal, maybe a predator.

It was the wrong thought to allow into my mind. Paranoia increased the speed of my footsteps until I was – once again – running like an idiot.

Lights shone from behind, and I heard the engine of a 4x4 as it approached and slowed beside me.

"What are you doing?! Are you mad? There is a pride of seven lions that feed in this area, elephants are all round you with their young, and you are about to walk straight across a hippo path.

You are a dead man, are you trying to commit suicide? Get in!"

It was Uncle Wency. In the story of The Valley, Uncle Wency is a lead character. A tall, dark man with a narrow frame and an oversized bald head, Uncle Wency was The Valley's local mechanic. He was also an adviser to all, a member on every committee, a self-proclaimed game ranger, a foul-mouthed drunkard, womaniser, and a knowledgeable and well-respected man. He was 'Uncle' Wency, because he was everyone's uncle, and despite his own wayward lifestyle, no person could ever argue against the honest and good intentions that Uncle Wency had for all people.

But I knew none of these things as we drove off in his army-green Nissan Patrol. I had no idea who he was or where he was taking me, where I would sleep, or what the next day would bring.

If you purify your Soul of attachment to and desire for things, you will understand them spiritually. If you deny your appetite for them, you will enjoy their truth, understanding what is certain in them.

- St John of the Cross

5

Paddling In The Same Canoe

Maggie's Place was the local liquor outlet and spaza shop, smaller than any corner cafés I've visited anywhere in the world. It was a primitive block of brick and plaster, crowned with wooden beams from a dead tree, topped with strips of iron sheeting for the roof. The building was big enough to hold about 20 adults at a squeeze, and that's about how many people were there when I arrived.

There was a simple wooden counter that faced the entrance, which my critical eye assumed was constructed by a novice with nothing more than a hammer and a few nails. It was a display counter that held loose cigarettes and candles, sweets, handfuls of popcorn, groundnuts and maize snacks in transparent plastic bags.

Presumably the same hand that made the counter also fitted two rickety shelves against the wall. Cans of Lucky Star pilchards, loose eggs, more transparent plastic bags – this time filled with cooking oil, salt, sugar, flour and Boom washing powder – some Lifebuoy soap, loose razor blades (the type that barbers use and not the 5-in-1 advanced formula that you and I might be familiar with), torch batteries, matches, empty bottles of Coke, Fanta, Mosi and Castle, and a few cosmetics like Vaseline, lotion and women's hair products filled these shelves. Although when I say "filled", I'm probably making it sound more impressive than it was as the shelves were just wide enough for a single row of products.

Uncle Wency greeted the frail lady behind the bar who coughed a lot, and then reached toward a chest freezer that stood behind us and grabbed two Mosi. Local Zambian music blared from an old Telefunken radio that resembled something I had as a child back in the '80s, as Uncle Wency led me to the pool table which practically filled the remaining space of the shop. With holes in its carpet and folded cardboard under its legs to balance it on a chipped concrete floor, the pool table was the central attraction of Maggie's Place.

And though the cue stick was one half of the original two-piece design, I felt safe; as if I could use the pool table to make friends. It was familiar to me and I was carrying enough insecurity and self-doubt for me to crave familiarity.

Uncle Wency set the balls, I broke, and play began.

Hours passed by and the small room slowly filled to capacity with men and children alike. Men came by to add their token to the line of tokens on the table waiting to play, and young boys eagerly gathered around to watch this strange visitor to their land decimate every opponent who dared challenge him. I was in my element and the cheers of "Champion!" spurred me on, not only in my pool playing, but also in my beer buying and drinking.

By the time I realised that Uncle Wency had long-since departed, it was of no concern to me because I had made a bunch of friends and we were all happy-drunk and loving each other with our minds not travelling further than the moment. It was good to not worry about where I would sleep, but to somehow have that security that all would be taken care of.

But it was a very drunken faith.

A knock at the door caused me to wake, and through blurry eyes I scanned my surroundings trying to fit missing pieces together.

I was lying on the floor of a concrete cell, three paces long by two paces wide, on top of my sleeping bag, with my head resting on a folded sweater.

There were no windows or air-vent, just pure concrete from ceiling to red cement floor.

My bones ached, my head pounded, and the knock against the metal door deafened me.

"Phirén! It's me, Peter!" (a funny thing about the Zambians that I discovered, is how they interchange their use of the letters 'l' and 'r'. In their local language, the meaning of words remain the same, so they apply the same principle, when speaking English. It's quite funny. Try it with your friend, Barry, for example)

Angry at being woken up and angry with my headache, yet confused about my surroundings and very aware of my alien status in an unknown land, I opened the door to find a young man grinning childishly at me with a blue plastic packet in his hand.

"Phirén, good morning! Do you eat porku?" Peter questioned and, before I could answer, he continued.

"My brother just killed this one and has given me a piece from the neck. We eat together!"

As it usually does, the pieces began to fit slowly together. Peter was a kid from the pool table who had taken to me more than anyone the previous night. He had appointed himself as my caretaker and was the one responsible for finding the room that had kept me through the night. And now he was at my door at the crack of dawn with a plastic packet that held a freshly bloodied piece of a recently slaughtered wild pig.

I shook my hangover away and considered the day I was walking into.

"You wash. I am coming." And with that, Peter walked away, leaving his packet of 'porku' behind.

My room was one of about 10 in a semi-enclosed

compound known as Cobra Guest House and the fence that surrounded the area was handmade from wild grass tied together in bunches, stacked next to each other and secured with rope and simple branches from any of the thousands of trees and bushes that filled The Valley.

As I stepped out from my room, I saw a group of women in front of me seated on reed mats, washing clothes in big plastic tubs of soapy water. My neighbour was next to me, sharing a meal with a child while seated on the step. And across the clearing I saw a group of men around a really old, blue Land Rover with no bonnet, peering at its engine with ever-evolving theories.

I asked for directions to the toilet and made my way over for my morning ablutions.

Two paces wide and two paces long, with a brick-sized hole in the bare earth at the centre, the toilet was enclosed with a wild grass fence similar to the one around our bigger enclosure.

I dropped my pants, squatted and opened my bowels as the warmth of the morning sun greeted my shoulders from the open sky above me.

Fuck! I heard that. I wonder how far it is to the bottom? If I knew the speed of falling poop I could easily calculate distance. I reckon that's about a second and a half between my ass and the splodge. That's quite a drop. How did they make this thing – how do you dig a brick-sized hole? I wonder how many people have dumped down this hole. I wonder what it looks like down there...

Before my mind could consider the pile of crap at the bottom of the pit, my attention was diverted by the flies that buzzed around, feeding on the faeces that clung to the edge of the hole where dumpers had not been so accurate in their delivery. I finally finished my business, ignored how I had forgotten to take toilet paper with me, pulled up my pants and walked out.

A barefoot young girl stood waiting for me, caught my eye and walked off just a few metres to another identical grass enclosure, this time with a tub of fresh water and a bar of soap at the centre instead of a brick-sized hole for a toilet. This was my bath. I smiled at her as she walked away to another daily and random act of service, and I continued that smile as I squatted on the ground and washed myself with that shockingly fresh water, under blue sky and radiant sun. I cupped my hands, dipped them in to the tub and then threw water all over my body before soaping myself and then repeating the process to rinse.

It might sound weird to you, but I truly felt that my life was richer after that morning ablution session; there was something about it that set me free, and if you were there, you might have noticed a brighter look on my face as I emerged and made my way back to my room.

Peter – who had returned from wherever he went – sat by my doorstep in fat conversation with my neighbour and, as I drew near, a girl arrived with firewood and an *mbaula*, and Peter began making the fire.

I asked him where I could find rice, vegetables, salt and cooking oil, and he instructed my neighbour to watch our fire while he took me to the market.

I feel badly trapped between two minds here. The people are so friendly and helpful that it seems like I'm being set up for a big con. I mean, it's just not natural and ... well 'they' do say that if it seems too good to be true then it probably is. So I really should watch out. But then it feels so good. It feels so REAL ... like this is the way of life that I so badly want to believe in. I so badly want to believe that we can be living in such unity and trust. But then am I romanticising this culture because it's not mine? Shit, I don't know. I have a good feeling and bad feeling all swimming around in my stomach at the same time. If I trust that all is good, then I could leave myself open to major pain. But if I doubt everyone when they're actually being genuine, then I could close myself off to really great opportunities...

As Peter and I exited the enclosure, I began to recognise a bit of where we were. It was what was referred to as the trading area of The Valley and we were adjacent to the tarred road and opposite Maggie's Place. In the daylight I began making sense of my surroundings.

There were several small buildings next to each other on both sides of the road, about ten in total, each about the size of a corner café. Three were incomplete; just a foundation, a few half-built brick walls and nothing else.

There was no grass anywhere, only naked earth (this was a decree from the chief, because poorly maintained lawn was more of an eyesore than bare sand), and behind the line of buildings was a forest of mango trees as far as my eyes could see. In the shade of these trees were countless rural settlements.

People moved around on foot or on bicycles, and while there were some vehicles, they were mostly branded with the logo of a tourist lodge.

We walked across the road past Maggie's Place, and I was a bit embarrassed by the many friendly greetings I received from men, women and children, because I wasn't sure if they were smiling at me or laughing at me from the previous night. We went behind the row of buildings and then reached the marketplace.

About 12 stalls formed something of a circular area that was squashed into a rectangular horseshoe with entrance and exit spaces on either side.

Each stall was made from dead wood, bark and

wild grass, and was big enough for an elderly woman and her young and barefoot girl-assistant. On the display area I saw onions, tomatoes, rape, pumpkin, pumpkin leaves, *delele* (okra), *kapenta* (tiny, dried fish, smaller than my pinky finger), live chickens, garlic, shelled groundnuts, salt, cooking oil, green peppers, empty 40-litre sunflower oil containers, and *impwa* (a type of baby brinjal, yellow in colour), which were mostly the items for sale.

I spent about 10 pin (six rand), which was an extravagant shop by Valley standards, and bought plenty of everything including a sunflower oil container, which was gently taken off my hands by a little girl. She walked with it to the nearest watering-hole, scrubbed it with soap and sand – which she used to replace the steel-wool that was necessary to get into all the spaces that the oil had penetrated – filled it with water and returned it to me at my room, where I sat with Peter and had begun cutting my ingredients.

That's how it was in The Valley, there was no running water. Boreholes with hand-pumps were randomly scattered around the area, and each morning every household sent their girls and boys to the nearest pump to draw water in plastic containers they carried on their heads back to their village to serve as their water for the day. *Manzi osamba* would be kept aside for bathing water, while *manzi okumwa* would be kept aside for drinking and cooking. There was always a long queue of kids around the boreholes, emphasising the shortage of clean water to the area.

My fresh pork neck curry was cooked to perfection and was exactly what my hangover needed. We ate until we could eat no more and then Peter sat back lazily to digest while my mind began to trouble me.

No electricity, no refrigeration – what do I do with all this leftover food? Maybe I relax and digest for a while and then we eat again ... I'm not sure...?

As if he had read my mind, Peter leaned forward and dished a healthy portion of curry and rice into my metal plate, which he then covered with his own.

"This is your food for before you sleep." He smiled

at me, "It is not good to go to bed hungry."

He lent back and put the plate in my room and then called out to the girl who had brought us the *mbaula*. When she came over, Peter thanked her and gave her my pot, which still had some leftover food in it. She took the pot and her charcoal brazier and disappeared.

Very confused, I leaned back once again.

"Phirén, now you rest. You drink too much last night and today you are tired. You sleep and tonight you eat and sleep again. I go now, but we are still together."

And just like that, Peter excused himself and walked away as I stared at him, slightly bemused with my unanswered questions still rolling around in my head. But my tiredness was stronger than my insecurity, and I soon crawled back into my room and passed out on the floor.

By the time I woke up, my pot was washed and returned, waiting for me outside my door.

As each day passed, my initial doubt softened. Strangers coming alongside to welcome and support me became such a normal thing that

I began to consider that perhaps there was no conspiracy. And as I took my eyes off myself and looked around at everyone else to see how they all interacted the same way with each other, the more my guard dropped.

This seems to be a genuine way of life here. People just look after each other – it's weird! I keep waiting for something bad to happen, but it doesn't. I just don't get it. Maybe if people were a bit more selfish here, then they wouldn't be struggling with poverty and under-development. But that's the thing, because life feels more real like this. I don't really understand it all, but I just know that it feels right inside my heart ... like it is something I'm supposed to learn from...

I spent my next few weeks intentionally trying to alter both my thinking and my daily habits.

Walking to the market one morning, I saw an old man stooped over a pile of dead wood by the side of the road. He was a short man, slightly built with bowed legs, and wore a face that carried the creases of many hard years. His grey hair was partly covered by a sweat-drenched cloth folded over many times to provide the padding for the load of wood he was carrying, but which he was bent over when I found him.

"*Ndo'kupya*," I said, taking the opportunity to practice the *Nyanja* language.

"Too hot." He responded, perhaps trying to impress me with his English, the same way I was trying to impress him with my primitive Nyanja.

"Where from?" I asked.

He pointed behind him into the distance and I saw a clearing of dead trees.

"Long walk," I replied.

"Wife. She's sick. What can I do? *Mkango ukasauka amadya udzu*."(literally translated: 'a hungry lion will eat grass', which means that regardless of who or what we think we are, when we are suffering, we will do whatever it takes to survive)

It took me a while to 'get it' but when I finally did I bent over, took half the load of wood on my shoulders, smiled at the *madala* (elderly man) and followed him home. I figured that to carry half the load was assistance, but if I had been so presumptuous to take the whole load, I would've insulted him. I don't know how I knew that, but it turns out that, culturally, I did the right thing. I think it has something to do with the pride of a man in a patriarchal social system.

I'm not sure.

We reached his hut, dropped the wood next to the fire, had a large cup of water each and I was off to continue my day, being carried by the blessing of an old man and his sick wife. I later heard news that she recovered soon enough and spoke frequently amongst her village of how the wood I had helped bring had kept the fire going for days, allowing her husband to stay by her side, which gave her the strength to recover.

That simple act of love and the effect it had on an old woman I had never met brought a smile to my face and increased my energy.

On another day I met a group of young fishermen. They woke up every morning with the sun to make their way down to the Luangwa River in the hope of catching some fish that they would spend the rest of the day trying to sell at the market. And sometimes, a fisherman could spend a whole day trying to sell just one bunch of fish, because each bunch was about 15pin (nine South African Rand), which was an expensive luxury.

That made no sense to me, because in my mind, it seemed perfectly obvious that everyone should be fishing and that fish should be the cheapest food item, since The Valley had a river running straight through it. But I had lots to learn.

Fishing in The Valley is done with nets about 25 metres long. Two men operate one net and both of them walk into the river together as one holds his position while the other moves out, slowly unravelling the net as he does so. There are only certain spots along the river where a man can do this without stepping into a deep patch of water and being washed away by the current. Then there are also the countless hippos and the largest population of Nile crocodiles outside of the Nile River to consider. These are some of the reasons why not everyone is a fisherman.

Nature has her way of keeping control, I guess.

Fishermen in The Valley are fishermen because they were born to fish, their fathers fished before them, and their fathers before them. It is something within them; their heartbeat. They have the ability to communicate with the river creatures, the ability to hear the nature of the river, the humility and obedience to not overstep any boundaries, and the courage to trust the art that has been handed down to them. And I respected this, so one day when I accompanied a group of fishermen down to the river to witness the poetry of it all, I was quite troubled in my heart by the nets they used, which were riddled with holes. I decided to travel to Chipata and buy new nets, which I donated into the village of the fishermen.

This brought great joy to the people, I felt appreciated, and my energy increased yet again.

I continued through random days like these for a few weeks and thoroughly enjoyed the beauty of them all. Each day and every person I met felt *real* and there was always a sense within me that I was being shaped into a better human being. And I guess I was, but I was also young and naïve with many lessons still to learn.

Four months passed, from the time I left home. Three of those passed in The Valley. And not for one of those days did I ever feel like I knew what I was doing. I just went along with the flow. Sure, I enjoyed every step of the way and I absolutely loved the culture shock, but there was always a concern inside of me somewhere.

I don't know what I'm doing here. I really don't. At times I think I'm supposed to be here to find work in a lodge or campsite so that I can sustain myself, but then every effort I make returns nothing and I end up spending my days in villages feeling more at home than I ever have. I keep meeting more Zambians and making more friends – people who genuinely care about me – and the more I engage with the people the more I feel that there is an incredible work of stripping-away that is taking place within me; that there is so much junk in my thinking that I have inherited and based my truth on, which is not actually truth at all.

I mean, like today I am walking along and then I hear, "Phireni! We are eating!" (a second

140

interesting thing about the people and their Nyanja language is how every word ends in a vowel. It is like the language was designed for speech alone, with the end of every word effortlessly flowing into the beginning of the next. The same principle was applied to English words, just like my name and Peter's "porku")

Like, what the fuck does that mean? So I look over and wave and smile and realise that I don't have a clue who the people are or why they're telling me that they're eating, so I continue walking. But then this kid calls out again, "Phireni! We're eating. Come."

I walk over and as I arrive this girl comes out from the hut and brings me a bowl of water to wash my hands in, space is made for me on the mat to sit, and I join these strangers and begin eating their very simple meal of nsima and delele (pap and boiled okra in a tomato and onion sauce). And while we eat, I ask questions and then I am enlightened about 'the Zambian way' – and it rattles my brain with its simplicity and truth. Zambians in The

Valley don't plan ahead. Planning ahead or looking into an uncreated future is not part of their conditioning – they are born; they eat, play and work in the fields; they marry, find some land and cultivate it together; and then they enjoy sex and raise children in the knowledge that they will continue the same trend. And as long as there is land for them to nurture and other people who make up their community, then life is good and there is nothing further to concern themselves about.

And it works.

I mean, these people aren't dressed in fashionable designs, their homes aren't very extravagant, they don't have swimming pools and shopping malls … but then I don't really see that they're missing much at all. The women aren't 'magazine quality', but that's not to say that there isn't an incredible beauty within them that is very attractive, even with their dirty, bare feet and sweat-glistening skin. In fact, life over here feels far more real and fulfilling than anything I've ever experienced in the 'developed' world.

It's weird. It's like a total dependency and trust on the Earth … and somehow, Mother Earth looks well capable of providing.

With the sun, stars and moon as my clock and calendar, time took on new form. And with the new perspective it brought came an uncertain certainty. I was not sure what tomorrow would bring, but I was sure that tomorrow was coming and that I would find myself at the day's end if only I persevered through all it had to offer; if only I just continued walking.

Back in South Africa, I think about money every day, it is an essential part of daily life. I wake up in the morning in a home that I pay to rent. I pay to use the electricity I need for the water my geyser boils so that I can take my bath, drink my tea, cook my food etc. I drive to work and that costs money, as does the majority of my communication with other human beings, because most of it is done via telephone, email or social media networks. When I am hungry, I buy food, and even if I choose to eat what I have in my little vegetable garden, I still use electricity to cook it. And then, of course, there are all the products that I buy.

143

And it's difficult to not buy things because I am bombarded with advertising every day until my brain eventually falls into some state of hypnosis.

I am very aware of money, back in South Africa, and I have a constant finger on the pulse of my bank account. In The Valley, however, things were different.

We had no electricity or running water, no radios, newspapers, television sets or advertising billboards. And the result was quite startling, because as these were removed from my daily life, the usual anxieties that I carry with me, concerning money – how little I have, how much more I need etc. – slipped out of my conscious thinking altogether. And with no place in my mind for it, my cash remained out of sight in the top pouch of my backpack in my room.

Wherever I have travelled, sampling the local flavour of marijuana has always been a highlight for me and, in Zambia, the *chamba* and the story behind it is a special one. Grown under extremely harsh and direct sunshine, the herb produces buds coated with resin as sticky as a lollipop that has been sucked by a child and left under the bed for the dog to lick. Once the buds are ripe for harvest, they are picked, packed into the dried skin of a mealie cob and buried about a foot underground, exactly where the goats urinate. The chamba is left to soak in the goats' urine for a few months, during which time it becomes as hard as a clay brick and as dark as fresh cow dung.

I'm not quite sure which brilliant mind discovered this process, or the scientific explanation behind it – I just know that it works extremely well.

Now, not everyone knows this art or has the discipline to apply themselves to the process, without getting high on their own supply, so the rastaman who did was highly regarded. Mavuto was one of these and he was my friend who stayed about a five-day bicycle ride away from The Valley, a trip he made once a month.

One of those trips was a fateful day for me that marked an unforgettable shift in season.

Mavuto arrived as usual, on his bicycle, gleaming with sweat, his dreadlocks tied up under his beanie. A man of peace, he was well known in the area and welcomed by all, so he rode straight into our enclosure, parked his bike next to the dead Land Rover and walked over to me with the smile of a friend. We greeted each other, he sat next to me on the step, pulled out some freshly harvested *chamba*, rolled a giant spliff, bumped his fist against mine, and our monthly fellowship ritual began.

It always went like that. We preferred silence, speaking only when we felt it was necessary. There was something about not needing to speak that brought us both a deep sense of gratification and peace, and those moments with the rastaman were always special to me.

Hours passed and eventually it was time for my friend to begin his long ride back home. I picked myself up and walked into my room to get some money.

"I must've been really hammered last night." I thought out aloud when my hand found only an empty pouch.

We both laughed.

"Man, be free." Mavuto replied. "We are still together. Next time is fine."

I smiled, went back outside, sat back against the wall and watched my friend ride away.

I drifted into a deep sleep that night, peaceful within the sounds of The Valley and safe in the knowledge that my money was somewhere in my room.

But it wasn't.

My initial panic lasted as long as the search of a single backpack can, during which time the thought of money returned with ferocity to the forefront of my mind. My knee-jerk response was that I had been conned, that the conspiracy was true, but that was a ridiculous idea because I had not allowed a single person into my room since I arrived. Then I thought I must have simply lost it somewhere, but that was equally implausible because the pouch it lived in – together with my passport – was all safe and exactly where it was supposed to be. Eventually, as I replayed my time since arriving in The Valley, I reached the conclusion that my choice to adopt a way of life that puts people first, not measuring my days' activities against my bank balance, meant that I had spent it all.

I have never felt so lost and without hope.

I didn't know how much of my own self-worth and confidence was attached to my financial status either.

I pulled out my journal and my pen and began to write, in the hope that some great wisdom would miraculously reveal itself.

I am miles away from the nearest telephone, bus station or internet access point; about an 8 hour ride with a Canter, to Chipata. Of course I could just walk back to Flatdogs, but that's not an option. I'd rather die than admit defeat and return to the capitalist world on my knees. The Canters only run once a week and the last trip arrived yesterday morning, so that's not an option. Besides, even if Kalyazi does me a favour and I can get to Chipata, I still have no money to get me further. I would need to sleep somewhere, eat something and still get to Lusaka before I could even think of getting back home.

What do I do? Where to from here?

Early the next morning, I left my room and set

off, all packed with nowhere to go and no plan on how to get there. But it was the best idea my broken mind could come up with; I had started the Journey by walking and it is walking that had sustained me through all the months, so when I found myself in a corner, walking was my only solution.

People greeted me, no doubt having heard of me and my many good deeds. But I did not return my usual smile, because I was cloaked in shame. Not having any money meant that I had nothing to offer, and having nothing to offer made me a liability – this was my inherited thinking and it tormented me. How ugly I felt at the thought of being a burden amongst a people already burdened with poverty. It was more than I could handle, so I summoned all my strength to walk as far away as I could from the place where I had become known.

The sun rose, the air hung still, thirst irritated my throat, sweat poured through my skin, hunger made its first announcement for the day, and eventually my strength left me.

I dropped my pack to the ground and sat down,

defeated.

"Where to?"

It was the question Africa threw at me whenever I was stagnant, shifting my mind into a much-needed direction.

I let out a sigh of resignation.

"I don't know. I need to get to South Africa." I responded, without looking up.

"South? Where from?" The toothless man who looked like a boy questioned.

"South." I replied, "I came here four months back from South."

"And now you are returning?" Bianda seemed perplexed, and an honesty in his eyes drew an honesty from my mouth.

"I have no more money."

That was the truth I dreaded.

My life's experience in western society has taught me that a person without money is a person without value, and a person without value is of no use to society at all.

It's an absolutely terrifying thought, when you think about it.

And I never knew how enslaved I was to this mind-set, how deeply ingrained it was in my subconscious, until I was forced to face the reality of it.

"Have you eaten?"

Bianda's question brought me back to reality.

"No?" I answered uncertainly, wondering where the conversation was headed.

"Why come to The Valley and then go home?" Bianda persisted.

That was quite a question.

In fact, it was *the* question. The question that unlocked my next season, that forced me to search my heart for the truth I had lost along the Way.

"In my heart I heard a Voice call me to Real Africa, and I have been following this Voice for months. This is how I reached here. But now I am lost, my money is gone and I need to get back home."

Bianda's whole being burst into a radiant beam of

light right in front of my eyes.

"Philén! Don't worry, we are paddling in the same canoe!" The man who looked like a teenager lifted his right hand to reveal a small plastic packet that contained about ten fish each approximately the size of my index finger.

"We have lunch, come!"

Bianda did not wait for me, and I was in no position to question what seemed like a pretty decent offer. I picked myself up and followed him across the ever-quiet and empty road until we came face to face with a high wall of wild grass that towered above me.

He stepped directly into it and disappeared.

I looked around, confused, for a moment, then I looked back at the wall of grass in front of me. Everything felt so unrealistic, like I was in the Truman Show, that eventually I decided to just step blindly where Bianda had gone. The grass wall closed behind me as I walked through, my feet found a well-trodden path, and a whole new world opened up in front of my eyes.

I moved slowly and soaked up as much of my

experience as I could.

I was surrounded by naked earth, deep brown in colour, with a hint of red.

Bare feet beat a steady rhythm into the ground all around me – running, walking, dancing, working. The feet of men, women, children, chickens, goats and cows.

Children followed us along intersections of winding paths as we walked. Some ran ahead and called out to their friends, others lagged behind and looked on inquisitively.

All around me were little villages of just four or five huts in circular arrangement, randomly scattered under the shade of mango trees.

I saw men seated under these trees, drinking, talking and laughing.

And I noticed fire pits at the centre of each of the villages, sending smoke into the air.

The picture was exactly what I saw and fell in love with on my first day on the back of the Canter, as we drove down the hillside from Chipata and into The Valley. It was everything my heart yearned for and grew so anxious about when I was at Flatdogs. It was the very reason I risked my life like an idiot, to walk amongst the wildlife that night I bumped into an elephant.

Real Africa.

My two guiding stars sparkled and I knew – even though I had no money and no plan – that I was exactly where I was meant to be. All that remained was to just keep walking and discover where the Path would lead.

In the old days, when we were young, the traveller through our country would stop at a village and he didn't have to ask for food or for water; once he stops, the people give him food and entertain him. That is one aspect of Ubuntu.

- Nelson Mandela

6

Ubuntu

I formed part of a circle of eight men, seated in the shade of a small tree. I was the youngest with the eldest being easily around the 60/70 mark. He sat on a stool next to me on my right and Bianda, with his toothless grin, sat on my left. The others lounged on a mat made from dried grass reeds, which began at my feet and extended in a rectangular shape big enough for five men to comfortably relax on, leaving enough space in the middle to serve as a dining area.

A bunch of young boys hung around us, a couple of them were up in the tree above my head with the others hovering on the fringes of our men's circle, listening in on our conversation, eagerly awaiting an instruction of any kind that they could race each other to carry out.

Our tree was the only one in a clearing of immaculately clean swept earth that housed a fireplace in the centre of a circle of six huts. Girls moved continually within the setting, sweeping the ground, tending the fire, sifting maize and groundnuts, deleafing and boiling pumpkins, peeling and roasting maize cobs, plucking chickens and busying themselves with all sorts of other chores that baffled my mind.

I looked around to try and see what the women were doing and noticed that most of them were either busy in their huts or in the fields tending to the fresh produce that surrounded the village similar to the way high walls and electric fences surround residential areas in Johannesburg. As I paid attention to the small fields of maize, sugar cane, sunflower and groundnuts that enclosed the village, I was deeply impacted by the healthy relationship that existed between the people and the Earth.

Real Africa.

When my eyes had finished racing around and my mind had returned to our circle of men, conversation began and it was all centred on me.

The well-respected *madala* of the village was

deeply intrigued by my story and how I had been led to his home by a mysterious Voice within me. And as his interest grew, so did the interest of all the others, who eagerly joined the conversation.

As we talked, girls emerged periodically from the huts with bowls that they placed in the centre of our reed mat. Some of these were filled with raw groundnuts, while others held strips of sugar cane and roasted mealies.

We continued talking, picking at the snacks as we did so, while some boys ran off into the distance and returned with a pouch of *balan* (locally grown tobacco leaves) and *chamba*, which one of the men hand-rolled in scraps of newspaper before setting it alight and passing it around.

And then an old and dishevelled woman appeared with a smile and a bottle of murky liquid (locally brewed 'wine' made from fermented maize and fruit) that she placed at my feet.

"*Zikomo kwambiri.*" (Thank you very much) I said in my simple Nyanja tongue that knew only a handful of words.

But my effort was appreciated and the old woman

returned my greeting, as the men in our circle nodded approval.

Bianda called out to his hut and a girl brought a 500-millilitre yoghurt cup to him. He handed it to me, decanted a healthy amount of 'wine' into it, placed the bottle back at my feet and stared at me with the eyes of a child who has given its mother a gift and is waiting for her to open it.

I took a puff of the heavily head-rush-inducing *balan/chamba* cocktail cigarette, passed it onto the *madala* next to me, downed my cup, refilled it and handed it to Bianda. He smiled, and there were many comments thrown around the group that made me feel right at home. I had done well. The air of discomfort that I had felt, slowly lifted and a feeling of deep relaxation came over me as I felt a sense of belonging right where I was.

I come from a world of television, newspapers, magazines, shopping centres, facebook, twitter, satellite television, fast-food outlets and microwave ovens. I am used to a world of isolation and seclusion, high walls and security gates, locked doors, email and text messages. I know much about the world where 'relationship' and 'community' are little more than words thrown around in sermons and presented in academic papers, conferences and workshops. And I have felt both the pain and yearning of my heart for something deeper and more authentic in my life.

Sitting with Bianda and his fellow villagers on that day freed my mind to the possibility that there was more to life than I was aware of; that the culture I had been raised and indoctrinated with was not the only way to live; and that there truly were answers to the questions I was asking.

Very simple answers.

I allowed my mind's eye to detach for a moment, to observe all that was taking place.

A group of men seated under a tree, at one with the Earth. No walls, no fences, no ceilings or artificial lights, no shoes on our feet.

Children gathered all around, listening, learning, laughing, growing.

Conversation centred on God, Spirit, Life, Love, Earth and Humanity.

No television, no radio, no newspapers.

No propaganda, advertisements, products, memberships, mortgages or vehicle repayments.

No noise.

Just people...

being people...

with other people.

Real Africa.

Hours passed and Bianda's wife eventually appeared from their hut, together with a train of girls following close behind. One by one they came to our circle and placed bowls of food on the mat.

There were some braised pumpkin leaves in one bowl and some *delele* in another, which was boiled with tomatoes and onions to make a sticky dish with the texture of snot. Bianda's fish were deep fried and crispy and added to a tomato and onion mix. And the last bowl set before us was the largest of them all and was filled with *nsima* (mealie 'pap' made from maize meal and boiling water), which is to Africa what pasta is to the Italian, or what rice is to the Indian.

Once all the food was placed in front of us, a young girl came to my side with a metal tub of water. I washed my hands and the tub was passed to the *madala*, then to Bianda and around the rest of the group. By the time the last man – presumably the youngest – washed, he was washing in a thin mud mixture created by seven pairs of very dirty hands that spent most of their time toiling in fields.

I was very intentional about observing the culture of the people and not causing any disrespect, so I held myself back and waited to see what happened next and what was expected of me.

Everyone reached out in unison toward the central bowl of *nsima*, picked a fat lump of pap and fondled it into a ball with one hand. I watched with keen interest as they pressed their thumbs into the ball to make a little depression, turning their ball into some kind of spoon, which they returned to any of the bowls of *ndiyo* (side dishes) to scoop up some accompanying relish before returning it to their mouths.

The process looked simple enough and I didn't hesitate to follow suit.

Thankfully, because of my Indian heritage, eating with my hands is something that comes naturally to me so it took only a few mouthfuls before I mastered the technique. This prompted a few words amongst the group, who were all expecting me to struggle culturally, and the *madala* even went so far to say that he was very grateful. He explained how the information he had heard about foreigners was that they were very intolerant of African culture, either isolating themselves from the people, or forcing the people to adopt their western ways. To have me sitting, smoking and drinking with them in their village was a very special thing, but that I was also eating with them from the same plate was something he did not expect.

I felt proud of myself for stepping out of my comfort zone, and how that small effort from me had positively impacted an old man. But at the same time, I couldn't help but feel embarrassed for how those who had gone before me had tainted the name of all 'foreigners', creating such a negative perception.

Thankfully, I was not given the time to lose myself in thought, because I soon noticed how a gentle silence had washed over us all, as eating became the main priority.

Where I come from, the *ndiyo* was probably enough for three, maybe four adults. It was certainly not enough for the group that we were. But I was not 'where I come from'; I was in a land far away, with people radically different, caught up in a lifestyle that challenged every part of my conditioning. It was a moment in time where I came face to face with Ubuntu.

An old man walked along the path that passed by our village.

He walked over to us, sat himself down, greeted, washed his hands and began eating.

I was shocked and astounded, but to everyone else, things were absolutely normal, and nobody batted an eyelid.

More men joined us and the pattern continued.

The bowl of *nsima* was plentiful, and each hand that dipped into it did so without caution, because there was no chance of it running out. But I noticed

164

something interesting as I watched each person scoop up some ndiyo. If it was the *delele* or the pumpkin leaves, each person literally dipped their ball of pap to just get a slight bit of the flavour. The same was done with the tomato and onion mix. But when it came to Bianda's little fish, whoever felt like a taste only broke off the tiniest fragment of flesh before adding it to his ball of pap, which was lightly coated with some sauce from the other bowls.

I felt ashamed.

Back home, whenever I eat, I stuff myself. I dish up huge portions of rice and meat, potatoes and veg, pasta and sauce, burgers and fries. It never crosses my mind to dish less, because there is always such an abundance. Watching how people ate with such consideration for each other, even strangers, was something that rocked my little brain. It is just not a way of life that I have grown up with, but it resonated within me, so I was very happy to immediately apply it.

Ubuntu.

Eventually, each of our actions grew slower and slower until – at last – we reclined, one by one with a look of deep satisfaction on our faces.

"*Wakuta, Philen*?" (Are you satisfied, Philen?)

This was the way in which the *Kunda* people (the tribe of people indigenous to The Valley. Originally a hunting tribe, these people have slowly lost their identity as the wildlife has become protected in National Parks) asked me if I had eaten enough. And boy, was I satisfied. I had eaten until I could eat no more, as had everyone else, and I smiled as I looked at the leftovers that remained, which the girls cleared away.

The day continued into night, drinking followed eating, smoking accompanied drinking, and singing, laughter and dancing blended us all into one.

When I awoke I was on the floor.

But so were the other two people in the room.

I was in a hut; a mud hut is how they are known amongst the English-speaking world, but that's not entirely accurate. The hut was made of river-clay bricks cooked in fire under the ground, the walls and floor were plastered with a mixture of cow-dung and clay, and the roof was a rural thatch-job made from bundles of dried grass.

I thought the design was ingenious, because it used natural resources in a non-exploitative way to create settlements that blended perfectly with Nature. To me – thinking about preserving the Earth so that our children get to enjoy the fullness of its beauty – it made more sense to construct these simple settlements and to merge humanity with Nature, as opposed to wiping out entire ecosystems to build residential areas, towns and cities.

Mud hut makes it all sound barbaric, but, in my opinion, it is very far from barbaric ... probably closer to intelligent than we're willing to admit.

I was in the middle of a hut on a reed mat on the floor, a teenage boy was next to me and another younger one was lying down lengthways at our feet. I stirred and moaned myself awake, and the teenager spontaneously arose and left the hut with a warm greeting directed my way.

A short while later, the little one followed him.

I was still trying to recall the previous evening when they both returned. The little one handed

167

me a pair of *tropicals* (slip slops) and the teenager invited me to take my bath.

Stepping out of the hut and heading towards my bathing area was the first familiar thing I did since entering the village the day before. The grass enclosure was the same as the one I became used to at Cobra Guest House, the floor was bare earth, the sky baby-blue and the sun was toasty. I stripped off my clothes and hung them over the edge, next to where a towel had been left for me. I could see everything and everyone, and they could see me, but only my head and shoulders. I exchanged a few friendly morning greetings with complete strangers before squatting down to soap myself.

The place smelled of urine.

And then it dawned on me that we had been peeing against the enclosure the night before. A million thoughts ran through my head, but when I saw that I was wearing *tropicals*, it all became clear. We pee'd against the outside at night, bathed on the inside during the day and as long as we did not confuse the two and kept our *tropicals* on, things were okay.

I finished my bath, clothed myself and started walking back to the hut. But I never made it, because I was intersected by someone who had heard of me and wanted me to eat breakfast at his village.

The story of a boy following the Voice of his heart and being led into the rural villages of The Valley spread like mist down a hillsides of Kwazulu Natal. I was taken from village to village, hut to hut, meal to meal and hand to hand, so that I could share my story.

There's something radically different going on here. People are more interested in my story than anything else. Everywhere I go, people are stopping me to ask questions. And we talk and talk and talk until they ask me to join them for a meal at their village, where we talk some more. And you know what's so whack? Not one person has asked me what I do ... like a job or career. Not one. And nobody has asked me about what I own or where I live or anything like that. Everyone is just interested in me and my story. It's totally fuckin' weird! I don't have enough money in my pocket to buy a single loose sweet, but nobody gives a shit. Nobody's asked about money. This Ubuntu thing is messing with my head, it truly seems much bigger and more capable than money. Man, I'm telling you that the more I get into this way of life and the more I understand it, the more I really start to question the western society that I come from, and the way of life we follow.

Could it be that Africa was closer to God before the religion of man was brought to corrupt the people and swing power away from the natives?

I thought I'd find all the answers on this Journey, but it turns out that I am just discovering more questions!

The second-hand of my internal clock fell away, the minute-hand merged with the hour-hand until my clock transformed into a calendar counting no more than days. Days became weeks, became months, became seasons until my concept, philosophy and understanding of time melted into an eternal horizon.

The secret of happiness, you see, is not found in seeking more, but in developing the capacity to enjoy less.

- Socrates

7

Real Africa

Maison Phiri is the second-born son of the late and former Chief Kakumbi, chief of The Valley. We met on a random day after word reached me and the people I was sharing stories with that the local wine stocks were low. So when evening came we all migrated from our very rural setting towards the slightly more developed trading area where electricity was sporadically available.

And we landed at Maison's place – a patch of earth he had acquired, which he fenced off with grass. There was a village-type ablution area in one corner and a simple building in the middle that was partitioned into three spaces – a tiny bar, hardware store, and bedroom – and stood just high enough for the average man to stand in without dipping his head. The bar area was about the size of Maggie's Place and housed a pool table and a rickety wooden counter. Behind the counter stood 10 cases of Mosi and a chest-freezer. And on the day that I found the place, it was filled with about 20 people.

I walked in and everyone noticed.

Maison, a tall and strongly built young man looked up, smiled a broad smile and came over to me with a Mosi.

"Welcome man. Do you play?" he said, pointing to his pool table which was in far better shape than Maggie's. There was a tone of youthful mischievousness in his voice which I enjoyed, so I decided to play along.

"Playing is for children, man. I don't play, I destroy." I smiled and he laughed.

"*Muntu wakamba*! (This guy talks the talk!) Let's play."

And that's how our friendship began.

We played and drank for five straight hours as everyone gathered around to watch, and Bob Marley and Tupac provided the backing soundtrack.

At last, when only a young boy and Francino the rastaman remained, Maison changed the course of our path.

"I'm sick of this shit, man. I'm getting bored of just winning. Let's eat."

We both laughed, and Maison called out to a young boy who I had noticed around us throughout the evening, busying himself with small jobs.

"*Jiros, pika nsima, mwana.*" (Jiros, cook us some pap, young man).

It took me a while to understand the dynamics, but when I did, this is what I learned:

Young boys in The Valley had very few choices available to them. They could either choose to remain close to their village, living the simple life, toiling as subsistence farmers all their days; or they could go to school, knowing that there was no option for tertiary education unless they left The Valley and went into town. And even after that, it was common knowledge that the job market in Zambia was pretty much non-existent.

Alternatively, they could find a role model; a young entrepreneur to work for and learn from.

Maison was the best role model a young boy could hope for, and many of them came by his shop to offer themselves as his servant, in the hope that he would teach them all that he had learned to make him the man that he was. And Maison was generous like that, offering as much as he could to as many as he could, as often as he could.

So when he instructed Jiros to cook a meal, it was perfectly normal. Jiros was new to Maison's home and needed to start at the bottom, cooking and cleaning. Over time, he would either quit and walk away, or he would be given greater responsibilities and opportunities, just like the many that had gone before him and whom Maison had empowered to take ownership of their own lives.

As Jiros walked off, Maison slapped me on the back and put his arm around my shoulders:

"Come. You will stay with me and Rasta, this is your home."

Behind Maison's hardware shop was the third part of his building, a shoebox-shaped room about as big as the spare bedroom of a poor man's house in the suburb of a developing nation. At the far end of the shoebox, was a three-quarter bed across the width of the wall, with a handmade wooden table next to it. A single foam mattress lay on the floor and an obliterated two-seater couch filled the rest of the available space.

Maison, Rasta and myself slept on the foam-mattress bed – head to toe – while Jiros and any other young boys who needed a place to rest for the night occupied the floor-mattress and couch.

This room was my home for a few months, and Maison, Rasta and Jimmy (whom I am about to introduce) became my brothers for life.

Although each day brought with it a new adventure, there was also a certainty to them that held all things together. Whether it was Maison, Rasta or myself who would stir first, as soon as we did, Jiros would immediately wake and exit the room.

If it was Maison, he would rise – never quiet – with a word, a punch or a slap, and a powerful stride outside to greet the day and all who shared it with him.

If it was Rasta, he would roll a mighty Marley in bed, light it, puff it and hand it over to me, who would wake instinctively at the sweet smell of the morning's burnt offering. We always took our time to enjoy that morning smoke before ambling

176

into the warming sun where we were sure to find Jimmy – our neighbour, with his peanut head and boyish grin – sitting in his mustard-yellow and army-green 1970s Defender 110, which was affectionately known as the *Bush Baby*.

The four of us usually chilled in the Bush Baby, reminiscing about the previous day and everything in it that had made us laugh. And as we remembered, we laughed again and again until Jiros arrived from the borehole and poured some water into the pot, which he placed on the fire that we kept perpetually alive.

Whoever felt most in need of refreshing usually announced his intention to bath at this stage, and then the remaining three searched mostly empty pockets for loose kwacha before ambling off to the marketplace.

Two pin usually bought a bag of *kapenta* or some eggs, a tomato and an onion and that was generally all we needed to accompany our breakfast portion of *nsima*, which we enjoyed with many friends in the shade of a simple thatch structure every morning.

Man, my mind has been rocked again! 'African time' is something everyone knows. In fact it is something that – I feel – Africa is mocked for. It's like Africa is so backward because Africans just can't grasp the concept of time correctly. I've even had this thought. I've definitely thought that Africa would be far more developed if everyone could just learn to be punctual! And I reckon it's true ... within a western context.

But my last couple of months in The Valley has messed with my thinking. I mean, I'm not in the western world now, I'm in Real Africa. And it's weird, because as time ticks by, my old way of thinking has slowly crumbled. It was scary at first, but now I'm digging it because it's helping me to see things through a wider lens.

Take food, for example.

In the western world ... the 'developed' and 'civilised' world where we are all so educated and intelligent, we eat our food from drive-thru's in the car, or in front of television sets, in conjunction with our work, in homes behind closed doors, high walls and electric fences.

We eat mostly hurriedly and away from the rest of our community.

But every meal over here is eaten amongst a group of friends and family gathered in a circle, sharing the same plates and spoons, cups and conversation in an accessible place so that any hungry passer-by can stop and join in for a meal.

Only in Real Africa have I found that any man is free to walk into another man's home at any time and to sit at his table to share a meal. And it is never an issue.

Now when I think about expenses that need to be met and budgets and deadlines and blah blah bullshit, it does make perfect sense that we should be more serious about our time. It makes perfect sense to grab a Big Mac and guzzle it down while I drive to my next meeting. But when I take my mind off the system that perpetuates fear and I think about those silly things like love, relationships, community, posterity, sustainability and all that 'nonsense', I begin to wonder whether Africa does not – in fact – have the answers we are all looking for in the self-help sections of the bookstore.

It seems simple. I guess it is. And fuck, people will probably laugh at me and dismiss me as an idle dreamer detached from 'reality'. But what if our reality is actually an illusion preventing us from living out the fullness of our humanity? What if we're actually supposed to be spending more time with each other and less time rushing around? What if 'African time' is something we're not supposed to change because it is actually supposed to change us? What would it look like if we were a world filled with people who took the time to sit down and share a meal with all those around us?

I spent almost every day after breakfast, either with Maison or Rasta.

When I was with Maison, I got to see the young and ambitious side of me; we talked about development and growth – the things we felt needed to be seen and the things we saw that were destructive to this dream. With Maison, 'impossible' was not a word in our vocabulary and we revelled in challenges, seeing them only as markers along the Way that revealed new strengths, skills and gifts to us.

We rode the back of the Canter trucks to Chipata to collect stocks of beer for his bar; paint, nails, iron-sheeting and PVC pipes for his hardware shop; and sweets, cigarettes, cooking oil and salt for ourselves.

We headed to the brewery to negotiate with Mosi suppliers to ensure that ample stock was always put aside for us.

We walked long stretches of road in search of dead trees to chop down and use for firewood at funeral homes, where we'd eventually land up sleeping on a reed mat outside by the fire until dawn.

And then sometimes we'd just hang around the pool table for the entire day, being boys.

When I wasn't missioning with Maison, I enjoyed chilling with Rasta by his little plumbing stall in the marketplace, listening to reggae and talking with the people.

But amidst all these wonderful memories and experiences, perhaps the one that most influenced my understanding of Real Africa is the wandering hen and her chicks.

They were everywhere.

Roosters, chickens and their babies all wandered around The Valley quite freely.

And that was a weird thing for me to see in such a Third World nation.

How could people just let their food walk around?

Were they not concerned that someone would steal them?

Were they not aware of how many lazy drunkards there were, who spent most of their days feeding from other people's homes?

Did it not cross their mind that these same people could quite easily pick up a stray chicken to take home and roast over a fire?

And who could say anything, because there was no way of identifying which chicken belonged to which person?

But it was never an issue.

And when I asked Rasta to help me understand the whole scenario, I was startled by the sincerity of his response.

"Man, if it is not mine, I don't touch it. I know the pain of being stolen from, the pain of being cheated, the pain of hunger that I do not deserve. I know these things. We all know these things.

"If I choose to steal another man's food, then I am choosing to hurt that person in a way I cannot tolerate myself. And if I hurt just one member of my community, then I am guilty of hurting the whole community. But I am a part of it, so to hurt the community is to hurt myself.

"Man, this is foolish. Even the dullest amongst us is able to understand such a basic principle. If we cannot trust each other, then what exactly do we have? No man, this thing you are talking is simply not in our thinking."

My time in the villages and amongst friends like Maison and Rasta challenged everything I had ever been conditioned with. And it is within this experience and that of the wandering hen and her chicks that I came to discover how Real Africa was never a destination I was called to reach. It is not a place and has no specific affiliation to any race, culture, language or anything else. It was simply the call of my heart to discover a life of Ubuntu.

Munthu ni munthu chifuka cha banthu. A person is a person because of people.

What I chose to do with that revelation was entirely my choice. But I was young, naïve and easily excitable, and I failed to consider how every 'heads' has a 'tails'; how every smile has a tear; how every friend has an enemy.

The Journey was far from over, and was setting up to take a turn for the worse.

Open your eyes and look within. Are you satisfied with the life you're living?

- Bob Marley

8

Elephants, Mice and Testicles

As I walked the Path with no purpose other than the Path itself, I engaged with some of the most memorable characters that a man could not possibly conjure up in his imagination. These are the people who took me into the wild heart of Africa to break down the last strongholds of my conditioning.

Deokrashas is my favourite of these friends.

I met him on a random evening at Maison's when we were hosting a pool competition and braai. The idea came to us on a day when Jimmy arrived from a visit to an uncle in a neighbouring village, carrying two chickens in each hand.

I loved that. People regularly visited each other's homes and – each time they did – they took a gift and returned with one. And these gifts were always as simple as chickens, beans or a small plastic packet of salt.

Ubuntu – it is more about simple acts of kindness towards each other than anything else.

Anyway, the pool competition was hot, the Mosi was plentiful, and the spices I rubbed on the chicken sent a flavour into the air from the fire that attracted the masses.

One of the many people I met that evening was a man who called himself Deokrashas.

He was a wiry looking character with a John-the-Baptist look about him; wild. He reeked of village-wine and balan, appeared to have never washed or brushed his hair in his lifetime, wore a shirt that had lost all its buttons and had no shoes on his feet. He was the kind of man I would never even have looked at, unless to give him a small guilt-offering of a few worthless coins. So when he invited me to visit him at his village the next day, I was excited.

Holy shitballs, this dude looks far out there! There is no way that there can be anything boring that will come out of this ... and what the hell ... if I am going to write a book then it might as well have some crazy peeps in it.

Rasta and Maison were still dead to the world when I awoke with Deokrashas on my mind. I knew it would be a nothing day as we all tried to recover from the previous night and when I surveyed the area and saw the cleaning that needed to happen, I decided to take Deokrashas up on his offer.

I stopped the first boy I saw, explained how I wanted to use his bicycle and proceeded to ride according to the directions I could remember.

The ride was long, hot, hard and dirty on a bicycle that felt like something my grandfather would have owned as a child, back in the early 1900s. I left the Kakumbi district and moved into Masumba, which was the area around the junction with the road that led to Chipata. After the first few kilometres of my ride that morning, my hangover sweated out of me and forced me to unbutton my soaked shirt. I continued to ride like this, looking out for an *mtondo* tree as I did so.

Mtondo is a word used in The Valley for a penis, so when you hear of a tree that is known as the *mtondo* tree, then you know there is a good story attached to it.

Also known as the Sausage Tree, it is an ordinary broad-leafed tree of medium stature that bears a fruit resembling a giant sausage or – as the Zambians so accurately observed – a giant *mtondo*. Although what is giant in western society is normal in African society, so you can imagine the size of the fruit.

Valley tradition has it that a man who desires a giant *mtondo* should visit a person with powers and ability to connect with the spirit realm and make his request. The spirit-person – after consulting the spirits of the ancestors and receiving guidance – then finds the right tree, with the correct young and small *mtondo*, which he marks before extracting some juice from it.

This juice is then rubbed under the foreskin of the small-penis-complex man, and the union made complete. As the tree's *mtondo* grows, so does the man's and when the man is satisfied that his *mtondo* is the right size, he returns to the spirit-person who chants a prayer of gratitude to the ancestors and then cuts the fruit from the tree to hand it to the man, who keeps it with him for the remaining days of his life.

If the fruit is ever removed from the sleeping place of the man, or if his waiting for growth results in the fruit ripening and falling to the ground, or if a baboon eats it, then there are unpleasant consequences.

Sickness and disease come upon the man's *mtondo* and from there it is entirely up to the ancestors to set him free or to destroy him.

Deokrashas told me to ride past the junction with the dust road from Chipata and to look out for an *mtondo* tree on the right side of the road, in front of a field of maize. He said that I would know I was at the right tree if I saw a young girl under it selling bananas. Just past the tree, if I looked closely I would see a space in the wall of maize that was big enough for a child to walk through. He instructed me to ride into that gap and trust that a path would open in front of me.

I found the girl, saw the tree and rode through the first gap in the maize field that appeared.

The footpath I found myself on, wound its way between the familiar small fields all scattered amidst the setting of villages that sat under a gentle cloud of smoke. Women and girls were wrapped in their colourful *chitenge*, either moving between hut, fireplace and borehole, or in the fields digging, ploughing, weeding and cleaning.

And the men and boys who were not being idle, where generally on a bicycle with a parcel of something – quite often charcoal – or seated under a tree.

Riding along winding paths between unfamiliar villages, lost in the beauty and serenity of the setting around me made it difficult to remember the exact directions I was given the night before. When I came to a T-junction with a short hedge in front of me, I turned right when I should have turned left. The path widened into a dusty road, turned around the corner and led me straight through a wide open gate.

My hair was wild, I hadn't cut nor brushed it in over four months, and my button-up shirt was unbuttoned and wide open, revealing fat beads of sweat dripping down a hairy chest towards my belly button.

I was the kind of picture that makes my mother

cringe, my father smile, and my brother wonder if we're related.

As soon as I entered the gate, I knew that I had made a mistake. I slammed on anchors and waited for the dust to settle.

A group of elder men sat in a semi-circle, facing another elder and respectable-looking man, and they all turned in unison towards me with startled expressions.

One of the men stood up and walked over to me.

"Where are you going?"

I briefly shared my story as I buttoned my shirt under the pressure of the gazes that had not left me.

"No. This is the chief's palace (pronounced: "chiefee's palace"). You should have turned left back there. Now go."

And then the guy who was dressed in a dark-green outfit turned his back and returned to the meeting with his 'chiefee'.

I rode away quickly, trying not to feel like an absolute idiot. But what I can say is that I have met Chief Mkhanye and all his village headmen, at his palace ... and that's cool.

Deokrashas saw me first and remembered me by name.

"Philén! Over here."

He was seated on a rough, handmade wooden chair in the shade of a small tree, and in his hands was another piece of wood that he was fashioning into an axe, using a piece of metal he had sharpened with a stone to serve as a knife.

I smiled, waved and rode into his village.

"You found me! Welcome."

His bearded face beamed light towards me as he called out to his hut in Nyanja, and a small girl appeared with a simple wooden stool and a folded reed mat. She unravelled the mat on the ground and placed the stool next to Deokrashas' chair, which he vacated for me.

We talked for hours – in a mixture of English and Nyanja – about the weather, the land, the crops, the rain and its seasons. We talked about women and politics and the difference between the white

193

man, black man and their life's philosophies, about fish and wine and a little boy who could not speak since his mother passed away.

As we spoke, I drew a chessboard in the sand while my friend carved its pieces from whatever stone and wood was within reach. When we were done, our attention switched to the battlefield of the board game, and conversation shifted to its similarities with life.

Smoke rose from a fire in the middle of the sandy clearing.

Young girls exited the hut at random intervals to check on a black pot that sat just above the flame, stirring it occasionally. Another girl, younger than a teenager, spent her time bent over, sweeping the clearing with a bundle of small dry branches tied together with a strip of bark.

Young boys mimicked Deokrashas and myself by sitting in the shade of another small tree talking aimlessly about the world, as young boys do.

A third girl returned from the distance with a plastic container filled with water balanced on her head as her little brother toddled alongside her clumsily holding onto a few pots in his hands.

And as I looked about me, the same stage act that was taking place in our little clearing was happening in every clearing as far as my eyes could see.

"Check," my friend grinned at me as he slid his knight into place, taking advantage of my wandering mind. I returned his smile, dodged his offence and took the burning cigarette from his extended hand, which he had been rolling while my mind was swimming in my surroundings.

I took a drag and sat back to watch Deokrashas ponder his next move.

The sun was overhead when the work of the women and their young girls reached completion, and it all coincided well with the rumbling of my tummy. My attention shifted – once again – to the activity around me.

First, a plastic jug of water and one drinking glass was brought out from the hut and placed on the reed mat at my feet.

Next, a basin of water was held out for me to wash my hands in. The girl who had been attending to the pot on the fire followed close behind – she came out with a plate heaped with *nsima*.

Two young boys with mischievous smiles brought out a pile of small metal plates, which they placed respectfully before us with excited giggles.

And finally two elder women emerged with a plate of fire-roasted village-chicken, a bowl of tomato and onion gravy and another with braised rape leaves.

One of the women faced me, did a sort of curtsey, clapping her hands together three times in a vertical motion before returning to the hut with the other woman and the little children following close behind.

"My wife," Deokrashas smiled at me with pride, and I returned his smile with a nod of respect as the basin was taken from me and placed in front of him.

As soon as Deokrashas had washed, I reached forward, broke a healthy lump of pap from the pile, rolled it into a ball, dipped it in the gravy and stuffed it into my mouth.

We left our chess game idle and conversation

reduced to silence as all our attention focused on eating.

Four more men joined us at random intervals.

Totally normal.

Eventually, Deokrashas saw my mind slip away, followed my eyes to the path of the setting sun, and knew that it was time.

"*Malume, tiyen'*." (Uncles, let's go.)

It was something about the culture that confused me at first - there was usually no explanation. In the society I grew up in, it is always necessary to explain myself, so if we were back in South Africa and I was in Deokrashas' position then I would say something like: "Hey guys, it's getting late and our friend still has to get back to his home, so how about we wrap it up?"

Although I probably wouldn't even say that because where I come from, we all have our own cars and are expected to take care of ourselves, so getting home would be my friend's responsibility and not mine.

But in this scene, I was the visitor and friend, we

197

were seated in the clearing at Deokrashas' hut, which gave him rank over everyone present, and he saw my anxiety about the setting sun and made a decision that everyone present was going to walk back to the trading area with me to deliver me safely to my resting place.

And so all that was required were two words: "*Malume, tiyen'*."

Deokrashas held my hand and led the way. It was uncomfortable at first and my mind tormented me with questions. How should I hold, what's the correct pressure, do I squeeze, do I relax, what's going on in his mind, what are other people thinking...? But I felt so afraid of causing offence, that I gritted my teeth and went along with it, because it was something that I had noticed was quite common, since I crossed into the country at Chirundu a few months back.

One of the *malumes* pushed my bicycle alongside us, another disappeared into a sugar-cane thicket and returned with a stalk for each of us, yet another lingered behind to collect groundnuts in his shirt to satisfy our munchies, and the last member of the group continued a conversation with an invisible woman whose voice was the only identifiable part of her and indicated that she was quite some way in the distance.

When we finally reached the tarmac, a little boy was already waiting for us with a bottle of wine that he'd been sent to deliver by the invisible lady. The *malume* who ordered it pulled five hundred kwacha from his pocket (less than one South African rand) and handed it to the boy who ran off to pass it over to the resident winemaker, and our journey continued.

By the time we reached Maison, we were all well tipsy, and the festivities continued late into the night until Deokrashas and the *malumes* disappeared from sight.

The following morning, I woke up and emerged from our shoebox room to find Rasta and Jimmy already in the Bush Baby, while Maison was taking his morning bath and Jiros had the pap on the fire. I joined Rasta and Jimmy only briefly for my morning smoke and then automatically headed towards the marketplace to find the eggs that I never delivered for breakfast. And if you're wondering where I got the money from, just remember that Ubuntu is bigger than the money we have in our pockets.

The walk from the market back to Maison's was a straight and flat road surrounded on both sides by sand, tall wild grass, mango trees and villages as far as the eye could see. This meant that anyone on the road at any time was always visible to either those who sat by the roadside and idled their time away, or to any other road traveller, either in front or behind. As I began my walk back from the market to Maison's, I saw the shape of a person ahead of me that piqued my interest.

Like the sail of a ship in an unsteady wind, a man made his way towards me wearing a dust-stained, buttonless shirt, off-white shorts with a large chunk missing that allowed his left bum-cheek to enjoy the breeze, and the trademark bare feet of a villager. I noticed something that resembled a knife or baby machete in his right hand and in his left was a bottle of wine which he passed to me as he grabbed my hand to lead the way.

It was Deokrashas.

"Elephant culling at the clearing by the second

bend. Rogue elephant. Wants to disturb the people in the village. No family to follow. Not good."

And that was all I needed. I handed the eggs to the next boy I saw, with instructions to take them to Maison. And then I was off with my crazy friend to an elephant culling that we expected to find in a clearing somewhere around where the river took its second turn inward from the game park.

"Where from?" I questioned, wondering how my friend had managed to go all the way back home the previous night and return so early the next morning.

"Just here. Mum's village is here. All my brothers, they are here. Only when I get married then I go to Masumba with my wife."

That made sense. What didn't make sense was the so-called elephant culling that I had just been made aware of, and that was what captured my attention.

I was not sure what to expect, but when we reached the spot there was no way I could anticipate what appeared in front of my eyes.

I could barely see the goliath of a mammal and I could not count the number of villagers who clambered all over it as if it was a grain of sugar and they were ants. But what assaulted my world view did not throw Deokrashas from his stride as he grabbed the bottle from me, took a hefty swig and turned to grin a maniacal smile before wading boldly into the swarm with his knife in one hand.

I don't think I could ever be able to convey the vivid scene to you, but let me try...

Pick any one of the historical war epics, like *Braveheart* or *Gladiator* for example. Now picture one of the war sequences where we are shown an open field with one army on the one side and the other army on the other side. Picture the two armies running towards each other, and finally get a clear picture in your head of what it looks like when they clash.

This was the scene that unfolded in front of me.

I knew it was an elephant culling because my friend had told me so, but if I was a stranger who happened to walk past unaware, I could easily have thought that two barbaric tribes were at war with each other. Knives, axes and machetes were wielded fearlessly and without restraint amidst a din of voices that were neither identifiable as jovial nor hostile.

Men retreated regularly from the centre of the action, covered in blood. They held large chunks of fresh meat in their hands as they did and as soon as their departure left a gap, it was filled by another who was waiting on the fringes to get into the mess. The retreating men handed whatever they managed to salvage to a boy who stuffed it in sackcloth before handing over a bottle of warm wine in return. The men gulped as much as they needed, as quickly as they could and handed back the bottle before re-entering the fray.

I sat in my spot of shade under a dead tree, smoking a *reefa* and enjoying the show.

When Deokrashas eventually removed himself from the crowd to make his way toward me, he had a fifty kilogram maize meal sack on his head stuffed with fresh elephant meat that dripped a wide trickle of blood over his face and onto his once-white-then-brown-but-now-forever-blood-red shirt.

There were two deep gashes – a knife wound across his left forearm and an axe wound to the skull above his eyebrow. The knife that went with him was lost in action, and that maniacal grin he had carried into battle was transformed into a broad and childlike smile of total joy.

"Crucial!"

That was all he said to me over and over at random intervals as we walked the five kilometres back to the trading area. It's as if – in the silence, under the weight of the sack and the hostility of the sun – Deokrashas was replaying the event in his mind, and each time he did so he reached the same conclusion:

"Crucial!"

I don't think I will ever know what he meant.

Somewhere between the trading area and Maison's place, we took a right turn and made our way into a village that I had not previously visited, and whose dwellers I had not yet met. There was a flood of mixed emotion, language, voices, conversations and instructions that rang out all at once as the little village experienced something that had never before been experienced in their history.

Not only was Deokrashas returning with 50 kilograms of fresh elephant meat, which was a great blessing seldom seen, but it was all happening together with me as their guest – the foreigner who looked like *Mwenye* (Indian), spoke like *Muzungu* (white man), yet lived with *Muntu* (indigenous African).

The village was different from where Deokrashas and his wife stayed. The setup was similar, with dusty clearings encircled by huts and a big central fireplace which served everyone. But this village lived under the perpetual shade of the giant mango trees that the elephants came out the national park to feed on.

Small boys spent most of their days in the trees eating mangoes, throwing mangoes, testing their climbing skills, swinging from branches, breaking branches and stockpiling large amounts of fruit for the wine-brewing lady.

And with Valley temperatures easily reaching above 40 degrees on a regular basis during dry season, this little village was perfectly located.

The sack of meat left Deokrashas' head and was handed to a couple of boys who went running with it into a hut, trailed by a group of excited girls, and I was taken by the hand to a gathering of elderly men seated under the central and largest of the trees.

It seemed that my presence in the village was of more interest to them than the meat, and by the look of pride on my friend's face as he introduced me, I felt that I was the greater of the two prizes he returned with on that day. And from what I had learned from the *madala* at Bianda's on that day when I ran out of money, combined with my many days with Maison and Rasta, I was not too surprised.

Visitors to The Valley usually landed at the small airport about 30 kilometres away, where they waited to be collected by a 4x4, which then drove them straight along the tarmac to their lodge, where they stayed until they left. It was extremely rare for any visitor to stop and engage with the people. It was also common knowledge that visitors came specifically for wildlife viewing and had little interest in the people who occupied the land.

"*Bwanji aKhulu.*" (Hello big man.)

"*Ye'o bwanji.*" (I see you, I acknowledge you and return your greeting).

Deokrashas greeted the elders and then introduced me as his new friend, which prompted a greeting from the eldest to me.

"*Mulimbwanji mZanga.*" (How are you, friend?)

"*Ndiribwino ka nawe aMdala.*" (I am just fine. How about you, Old Man?)

During the previous months I observed two different greetings. There was the way that was used amongst the younger generation, which was very jovial and informal and went something like this:

"*Atibwanji mwana! Mwadeera?*" (Hey, how's it going, man. Are you cool?"

"*Ah, niriche moshe. Uriche?*" (Man, I am just super cool. What about you, are you cool?)

"*Cha' bwino.*"(I'm just fine. All good.)

And then there was the far more deliberate way that I observed amongst the elders.

I chose the formal way.

I gently clapped my cupped hands together in front of me and then held them together for a moment as I offered a very slight nod of recognition and respect.

I did well.

The old man turned to the second eldest who was seated next to him, and the man vacated his seat and offered it to me. I knew I was in for quite a day when I – once again – took my place at the right hand side of the village elder.

Each piece of land has a designated chief, who is the overseer of the whole chiefdom. Each chiefdom is then divided further into smaller areas, and these areas are watched over by headmen, who meet with the chief on a regular basis to act as his advisers. This was the meeting that I stumbled upon at the palace of Chief Mkhanye, when I rode in with my shirt wide open.

Anyway, each area that is overseen by a headman is made up of several villages, with each village being between six to ten huts each keeping about four people. And within each village, there are the elders who are the most respected amongst the families.

It is these elders who fed information to the headmen, who returned it to the chief. And I was seated amongst them, on the right hand side of the eldest of them.

For a while, no words were said, we all simply sat in the moment and enjoyed it for what it was. While we did this the wine arrived, together with some *balan* and *chamba* and I knew that the rest of the day was not within my control when the eldest of the group poured his cup, downed it, poured another and handed it to me.

I downed it, smiled at the man and poured an equally loaded cup for the next person. And so it continued until an *mbaula* was brought by a young girl and set in the midst of us, burning with red-hot coals. Trailing close behind followed another three girls each carrying a metal bowl filled with elephant meat.

The bowls were set in front of the *madala* and

the girls retreated with a curtsey. The old man smiled at me, thanked Deokrashas, reached into the middle bowl and removed the beast's liver. Culture required the feet, trunk and penis of any elephant culling to be delivered to the chief, after this the liver was a much-revered piece that usually went to the village elder.

So as much as the *Braveheart* frenzy in the open plain that morning had been about food, it was also truly a battle for the feet, penis, trunk and liver, since these treasures won a man much favour amongst the leaders of his people. And Deokrashas had succeeded with one of them, which we all marvelled at while we waited for the feast to begin.

The *madala* sprinkled some salt and threw the liver directly onto the burning coals to sear it. He removed it by hand to take a generous bite, with delight painted unashamedly across his face.

Then he handed it to me.

What about hygiene? What about disease and sickness? How do you know that it has been thoroughly cooked? Is it safe to eat directly from the coals? How clean are this man's hands? How do you know that you can eat the liver of an elephant? But there is still blood in it...!

The war within my mind raged.

The part that has been conditioned by western philosophy assaulted me with fear, doubt and a torrent of negativity that threatened to stagnate me. Every concern was legitimate, but was it relevant to my life and the Journey I had chosen to undertake in pursuit of Real Africa?

I decided it was not.

This community was well and healthy – raising children, caring for the elders, nurturing the land and loving each other – long before I ever arrived, and would continue well after I departed. I was nothing more than an arrogant fool to think that 'my' way was any better than 'their' way. To be handed the liver by the *madala* at that time was an honour I was not willing to let pass by.

I took the meat from his hands and sunk my teeth into it for a large bite. Blood trickled down my chin, I wiped it with the back of my hand, passed the liver to Deokrashas, poured myself a full glass of village wine and downed it.

The festivities continued well into the morning hours, and it was a few days that passed before I decided to leave the village and head back to Maison and Rasta, where I took my time to ponder my experience and write in my journal.

If there are human beings who are living like this, then I will live like this and learn from them. This was my pledge when I started, and I will not back down. Man, I have eaten the fresh liver of an elephant, braaied goat's testicles, which tasted like smoked soya sausage, and this thing called mbewa. This little field mouse was boiled ... hair, head, guts and all ... and brought to me with a bit of salt. I couldn't believe it! I thought the people were joking, but then an elder woman came and explained how this was a traditional meal from as far back as she can remember, during the season when maize is abundant. She put the boiled mouse in her mouth and ate the whole bloody thing ... so I did the same – it was crazy! Didn't taste very good and I don't think I'll eat it again, but damn, it was worth the experience.

My mind screams at me, warning me about all sorts of diseases. Do I trust my mind and what it has been conditioned with by a world obsessed with consumption and profit, or do I trust my experience, which nobody can question? I don't know. I'm just going to continue walking this Path and if I die of some bad-ass disease, then I was wrong. But if I continue to live in good health, then the conditioning of my mind will surely be stripped away and replaced by the truth of my own life experiences.

Only time will tell...

Man.

Because he sacrifices his health in order to make money.

Then he sacrifices money to recuperate his health.

And then he is so anxious about the future that he does not enjoy the present; the result being that he does not live in the present or the future; he lives as if he is never going to die, and then dies having never really lived.

> *- The Dalai Lama, when asked what surprised him most about humanity.*

9

Muzungu

In Zambia it is commonly accepted that the word *muzungu* refers to 'the white man'.

But not in this book.

In fact *muzungu* – for me – has nothing to do with any specific race or people.

Nothing whatsoever.

And I first began to see this when I found myself sometimes being referred to as *muzungu* by indigenous Zambians, especially the children.

How can muzungu refer to a 'white' person, but still be used on me? Is there something more to this that I am missing?

As I allowed my mind to probe this question, new discoveries emerged until, at last, I was able to formulate my own understanding.

Muzungu is not a person or a place; it is not something tangible. In fact, *muzungu* is a pattern of thinking that establishes a certain mind-set within a person. When a person allows *muzungu* to control their thinking, that person then becomes an image of *muzungu*. Similarly, when *muzungu* is adopted as the prevalent mind-set of an entire nation, then that nation is said to be a *muzungu* nation.

In the same way that I discovered Real Africa to be more than a destination – bigger than a place, race or people – so too did I discover *muzungu* to be a pattern of thinking, furiously opposed to the way of Ubuntu.

Muzungu is the thought in our minds that begins with 'I'; it is fiercely independent and self-absorbed, materially focused and spiritually disconnected.

Muzungu is financially motivated, trusting in economic systems for security, rather than healthy relationships.

Muzungu is a mind-set that believes in ownership above sharing.

Muzungu is the voice within our minds focused on survival through oppression; it has no greater purpose than to establish its own empire at the cost of everyone else.

Everything else.

Muzungu is the way of life that leads mankind to destroy the Earth for our own fleeting gain – to wipe out land and put up non-sustainable structures, to destroy entire ecosystems to feed bank accounts.

Muzungu is the dark side of our inner battle, short-sighted and incredibly selfish.

I was raised in a *muzungu* world, conditioned with *muzungu* thinking, and had lived most of my life the *muzungu* way. Even though I had chosen to walk away in search of an alternative lifestyle and had fallen in love with Ubuntu, I was foolish to think that there would be no backlash. Even though I was oblivious, *muzungu* had never left me and was waiting in the corners of my mind for a gap to attack.

Mulonga Camp was the first tourist camp in The Valley, situated just splashing distance from the Luangwa, with clear sight across the river and into the National Park. Mulonga was the prime spot in The Valley for tourism, and it was also the only camp owned by a local Zambian. As I decided to move my Journey closer towards the wildlife of Africa, to get a glimpse into the world of tourism and travel, both Maison and Rasta directed me to Mulonga.

"Man, there you will find everything that the tourists come to see, all the wildlife you can dream of. But you will still be amongst the local people, so don't worry."

Time had come for me to move on and, once again, I threw my backpack over my shoulders and began walking.

Although it was the most perfectly situated piece of land I had ever come across, and filled with potential to be one of the great attractions for any traveller in search of wild Africa, Mulonga had the feeling of a place that had suffered the collateral damage of a war.

As I came to the end of my walk along the dusty road that led into the campsite, I was shocked at the condition of everything. Where there should have been beautiful green lawn, I saw overgrown wild grass. Only three of the six chalets were completed, but monkeys chased each other on the rooftops, pulling out large chunks of thatch that left gaping wounds for rain and insects to move freely through. The other chalets were just a few unplastered walls and empty window frames. At the centre of the lawn area was what I imagined to be a beautiful thatch shelter for spit-braais, except that it was only a concrete foundation with six upright poles and nothing else. The dining room was a shell of a building, and what could have been the most amazing bar, blended into a giant *msikizi* tree, was nothing more than a half-done thatch job, shading an unfinished concrete floor.

The place was a mess, and as I gazed around at the state of the campsite, *muzungu* began to surreptitiously sow its seed within me.

Mulonga was run by Chiyeso, who was the son of Bwana Chata, some influential politician in the Eastern Province.

Chiyeso was assisted by his spectacled cousin, Mwiche – a romantic poet, lost in a family of politics and power.

Mr Ondya was the caretaker, who lived in what was originally intended to be a storage room, built entirely out of aluminium.

Mabale was a very simple villager who was the odd-job man.

And Danny Wamba was Chiyeso's friend, a man renowned from The Valley to Chipata and beyond, for his insatiable appetite for sex and alcohol.

He once remarked – over breakfast – of his own sexual prowess:

"Man, when I'm having sex there are no rules. If you come into my room after I have finished you will find the mattress on the floor, the bed upside down, clothes are missing, and pillows … don't even talk about pillows!"

Despite the pathetic state of the campsite, the location was perfect and I took advantage of it by setting up my tent just five metres from the water's edge, where crocodiles sunbathed and hippos wallowed. There was a deep serenity about the place, and the force of nature was so overwhelming that I had no choice but to adapt.

Each morning began with the sun knocking on my

tent as the sound of night insects were replaced by the collective song of birds.

I would rise gently and emerge from my tent, listening to the silence of the river as it ambled past, while the rest of creation awoke, stretched, yawned and sang to each other.

During the night, the hippos left the water, walked up the bank past my tent and on towards the swamp behind the campsite where they spent hours feeding. Just before sunrise they returned so that by the time I awoke I found them already in the water preparing for a day of sunbathing and swimming. Their giant footprints in the sand just next to the water created the perfect natural toilet bowl, and every morning I walked over to one of these, dropped my pants and took my morning dump in a setting of pure harmony.

Ahead of me the hippos quietly shuffled around.

Across the river, impala and puku grazed amidst thick bush.

And in a tree above them the resident fish eagle sat and called out to its mate who returned the call every morning from the same place somewhere deeper within the bush that my eyes could not see.

When I was done, I covered up my mess with sand and made my way to take a bath. This was my morning ritual for a few months, and it was beautiful, refreshing, renewing, purifying, humbling and just plain awesome.

I discovered a completely new system of time at Mulonga.

Breakfast was always signalled by the first rumblings of the hippos. I never did figure out what they were doing, but it sounded to me like one of them cracked a joke upstream that prompted a gradual flowing of laughter all the way downriver. It happened every day at about the same time that all of us felt the first pangs of hunger.

Mid-morning was signalled by the second rumbling of the hippos sometime after breakfast and before midday, which was clearly identifiable by the overhead sun.

Every day, sometime after lunch and before sunset, during that period of laziness when we would all prefer an afternoon nap, three elephants

– a mother, her baby and a teenage male – crossed through the river, out from the park and into our campsite to feed on pods from the trees that provided us with shade, before continuing on the path that would return them the next day.

Sunset followed a few hours after they left, and then it was night.

Initially my mind rebelled against this new system of time; it was just not calculated and analytical enough. It was too free. But after a few days, my thoughts subdued and I grew more aware of a lifestyle radically different from what I had been used to.

A lifestyle infinitely more peaceful and natural.

It just felt right … besides that, it was a life filled with funny people.

My earliest memory of Ondya was of him sitting on a brick around a small fire the same time the elephants came through camp. Ondya instinctively shouted at the beast and attempted to establish himself as the dominant species. When the elephant ignored him and continued to feed, about 20 metres away, Ondya grabbed his handmade catapult and began firing tiny pebbles at it. I'll never forget the image of this simple man wearing nothing but torn shorts, continuing to fire his stones while retreating from the angry mammal as it mock-charged him and trumpeted its discontent.

Mabale on the other hand was an even simpler villager from north of the Luangwa Valley, where humanity was more rural than any settlement I managed to reach on my trip. He spoke no English, and even his thoughts and ideas expressed in his native Kunda tongue were as simple as that of a child. I always laugh when I think about the conversation we once had with him regarding sex, unwanted pregnancies and diseases.

It was an ordinary evening and we had all been drinking, and we decided to ply Mabale with some alcohol, for our own amusement. After a few swigs of the local wine, he dropped his guard and became quite jovial and talkative, deciding to share some of his life's troubles with us.

His greatest concern was how, by following his natural instincts, he produced more children than he wanted or could care for. He also complained bitterly about sores that affected his manhood, and cursed the *mahule* ('bitches' – this is literally how the people referred to women who seduced men for food and shelter) who brought him such problems. When we asked if he was aware of condoms, he replied positively, but when we asked if he used them, his stuttered reply came from a shy and child-like smile:

"*No, no, no. N ... n ... n ... niskini to skini, bwa ... bwana.*" (No, no, no. I like it skin to skin, big man.)

This cracks me up every time I think about it, but there is a lot more depth to this topic than meets the eye.

But I'll save it for another day.

I met Bwana Chata, Mulonga's owner, on a random day after I had taken a walk to the market to buy some food. Along the way I intercepted a few fishermen, one of whom had a healthy-sized catch of something I had not previously seen. He told me it was a bottlenose and was the tastiest of all the fish in The Valley. It looked decent to me so I bought it for *10pin*, took it back to camp and baked it in foil on the fire with garlic, black pepper, chilli, tomato and some *impwa*.

It turned out perfectly.

Just as the sun signalled time for lunch, Bwana Chata – a fat man with an uncomfortable, limping stride – arrived with some guests that he was trying to impress, and my bottlenose meal was taken by Chiyeso directly to them – a move that marked yet another change of season along my Path.

It so happened that my meal was the best meal Bwana Chata and his cronies had ever eaten, and that sparked a discussion, which culminated in me being invited to the bar for a drink with them.

They were all convinced that the food I had prepared was unparalleled amongst the local Zambians and that such a service, if offered to local people would help elevate the camp to international standards. I was asked if I would be head chef to use my cooking ability to help turn Mulonga into an income-earning facility, and I gladly accepted.

Cooking is something that pumps through my veins, it is a passion and a joy, so the idea of developing this as a career while living in the midst of paradise struck me as the greatest opportunity I could ever receive.

And it started off really well.

Bwana Chata and his mates returned to the towns and spread the word about the best cuisine in The Valley that was on offer at Mulonga, and slowly the traffic began to trickle in. Each weekend brought a group of upper-class Zambians to camp, and each weekend I delighted them with my cooking.

Wild pig curry and beans; baked bottlenose with garlic and black pepper; hippo steaks with stir-fried vegetables and a marula sauce made from fresh marula fruits I picked off the ground; and peri-peri grilled village chicken with a touch of something sour that I had found but which was not lemon.

I was in my element, and each visitor to the camp left so happy that they sent friends to us the following weekend.

And so it went.

Looking back, it was a life I could have lived with great joy, but *muzungu* in me would not let it be.

When I cooked that first bottlenose, it was done with no agenda. I simply saw something in my mind's eye, enjoyed the idea and pursued it to see if it would return as much joy to me, and bring as much joy to others, as I had envisioned.

And when it did, I felt good.

The first few meals I cooked, I cooked straight from my heart. I was so grateful for the opportunity, that I poured my energy into each day, trying to be as creative as I could, to bring as much joy as I could, to as many people as I could.

But *muzungu* changed that.

What if I turned the wrecked dining hall into a restaurant? I could easily get Bwana Chata to give me that portion of the camp for my own income and then he would benefit from my food and could use the interest of the people to help rebuild his piece-of-shit campsite. The camp would then depend on my food and I would become a major player. Maybe one day I could even own the camp.

High on my own little ego-trip, I approached Bwana Chata with my proposal, which I cleverly constructed with alluring sentences, to entice him. But to be honest, he didn't need much enticing. He took the bait without a blink of the eye and said that the kitchen and dining room could be mine as long as I provided the equipment.

And so began my unravelling.

My heart's call of Real Africa faded into the background, Ubuntu became just another part of my story – a closed chapter – and *muzungu* took centre stage.

Food changed from being a gift of the Earth to a resource useful for profit.

The kitchen moved from being my creative space to a workplace.

The people became customers,

the art became a process,

the meal became my product,

the joy became my stress,

and I became a *muzungu* man.

The hippos still called out the time,

the fish eagles still chatted every morning,

the elephants still visited each afternoon,

but I grew oblivious, as my thinking focused more and more on ownership and profit, and my selfish desires disconnected me from the abundant life I had just discovered and fallen in love with.

Every restaurant needs a bar, and though Mulonga had that, it needed an investor. The Boss was a key figure in the business world of the Eastern Province, residing in the nearby town of Katete. And being as connected as he was, it did not take long for word to reach him about the resurgence of Mulonga and this chef extraordinaire who was at the heart of it all. He promptly decided to seize onto the business opportunity and sent his trusted friend, Jerome '*The Lobengula*' to set up and run the bar.

A short, stocky fellow with a strong chin and a solid head portrayed a very capable man who held no fear for anyone or any work. But The Lobengula's smile, the kind that will cause you to burst out laughing in even the most distressing of situations, was the reflection of his heart that drew me in from the start.

We spent a few months together at Mulonga, during which time we were inseparable. We slept together in a three-quarter bed (a very common, un-homosexual thing similar to the holding of hands), woke together, walked to the market together, cooked together, sat in the dilapidated thatch structure that was the bar, during the afternoons together, and spent many hours talking about life and the dreams we had for a better future. And it was The Lobengula who christened me with the name 'Zulu', a name that remains even until today.

Like most of my friends along the Path, The Lobengula's history was filled with amusing stories.

When he was young, he heard of a precious stones supplier in Mozambique, who sold a product fetching a great price on the Zambian black market. He convinced his mother of his idea to trade in this commodity, borrowed the family's only bicycle – which is a big deal in a world of no motor vehicles – and headed off to Mozambique, about 100-kilometres away, with all of his family's savings.

He was gone for about six months before he returned with a massive smile of success.

The money he had taken was not enough, but he was so committed to the task that he had decided to trade the bicycle and return home on foot. And it was all worth it because he had found what he was looking for, which would repay his family's savings, replace the old bicycle with a new one, and send his little sister to school.

His father waited eagerly to see the precious stones he had heard about, dreaming of financial freedom, but was absolutely shattered when The Lobengula emptied his pockets.

"Precious stones," he said excitedly.

But his father did not share in his excitement. In fact, there was a look of sorrow, grief and desperation that washed across his face, as he informed his son that what he had sacrificed his family's savings and assets for was of no more value than the torn shirt on his back.

After this The Lobengula was sent to seminary school to follow in the footsteps of his brother. Thankfully, though he completed successfully, he rejected the idea of a life as a Catholic priest and ended up spending his days with me at Mulonga, growing a friendship that has become a lifelong treasure.

But the Mulonga dream was shattered after only a few short months, and it all hinged on the fact that the presidency had changed hands – Fredrick Chiluba was out, Levy Mwanawasa was in, and the consequences were radical.

"Man! Quick, let's go."

The Lobengula was laughing aloud in his high-pitched, boyish chuckle as he grabbed my hand and turned me around, but from his stride I could see that he was very serious.

I had taken a trip to Chipata with Maison a few days earlier to visit a friend he wanted me to meet, and was walking the five-kilometre stretch back to the campsite when I bumped into The Lobengula.

"Man, did you know that Chata was connected with that Short Man (referring to Chiluba)? Well, did you know that Bwana Chata has no papers for Mulonga? Nothing man, just imagine! So I find out now that Chata was very influential in canvassing votes for Chiluba, so when that Short Man became president he took Mulonga away from the owner and gave it to Chata.

"Just imagine, all this time Chata has been showing himself as if he knew what he was doing, but man, that guy has never known anything. Mulonga was just a payment for the job he did in getting Chiluba into power. But now the tables are turning again. I was sitting at the bar, man, and these guys from ZAF (Zambian Air Force) came in with this other guy and they started drinking. Man, they hammered the Mosi like nobody's business until we ran out of stock! And then they switched to the Bells. Eventually I could see this was going to be a problem so I asked if they could settle half the bill before continuing and then man, it all started.

"The other guy is one of Mwanawasa's people who helped him get into power and now Mwanawasa is giving Mulonga to him! And the ZAF guys are just there for the beer. Man, I tried to explain that I was only there for some short time and that Chiyeso and Mwiche were away, but were the responsible people, and I tried to mention about

The Boss and his business, but they were not listening. Man, I'm telling you they chased me! I had to leave everything, all the stock is still there and they are busy hammering it right now. It's a good thing you took your backpack with you when you went with Maison, because when I tried to get my things they refused. Man, they chased me from there without even letting me get my toothbrush. Just imagine, man, not even my toothbrush!"

Uncontrollable laughter erupted like it does amongst young boys who find themselves in an unavoidable and sticky situation.

A straight dusty road with dry African bush as the backdrop, a thin brown man and a short, stocky black man with no shoes on his feet, walking hand in hand under a shower of laughter. It was the perfect picture to the end of one chapter and the beginning of another.

We spent the night at Maison's and, during our night-long brainstorming session, I learned how fuel was a valued commodity, always in short supply in The Valley. As the topic came up, The Lobengula told me of a guy he knew in Chipata who worked at a filling station and who had a way into the system. The owner of the station was a Muslim man who also had a lucrative transport business, in fact it was his own trucks that were his major concern and the petrol station was simply there to ensure that he received the cheapest fuel while also getting some pocket money for himself.

Whenever his trucks came to fill up, no cash was required, the drivers simply completed the necessary paperwork, received a full tank of fuel and continued their work. Somehow it all added up in the end when the mileage book was checked against the fuel records.

But there is a loophole in every system, and for those who work within it and are oppressed by it, it is always a glimmer of hope to exploit.

As I sat with The Lobengula on the back of the Canter at midnight, heading to Chipata, he explained everything to me. He told me how truck drivers never took the shortest route; how their lives were all about driving and how they enjoyed trying to get the most mileage out of every trip. He also explained how the truck owners knew none of this, because they spent all their time sitting at home and in their office, counting their money. And as long as there was profit, they couldn't care about what was going on behind the scenes.

But as the Canter bumped along the gravel road, and we bounced up and down on the bare steel back of it, the plot thickened.

The Lobengula's friend at the station had a cousin who was one of the truck drivers. The plan was for him to fill up his truck as usual, making sure all the paperwork was in order. We would then be informed of the route the truck was taking and would intercept it along the way, siphon out a full drum's worth of petrol and then head back to The Valley with this drum while the truck continued its journey. The driver would shorten his route to ensure that no discrepancies were found in the owner's profit margins, and we would make payment in cash to the friend at the station, who would split the takings with his cousin. The price we would pay was considerably less than the consumer price of fuel, which would allow us to resell it in The Valley for a worthwhile profit.

Win-win.

And as we rolled it out, it all went perfectly according to plan and we were back in The Valley within three days with a drum of petrol that we stored in Maison's hardware shop.

Word spread fast and within five days, the petrol was finished. And so began the first successful business of The Lobengula and myself.

But Ubuntu thrives on loving kindness and positive relationships, while *muzungu* depends on financial profit alone. So as these two philosophies came head to head in our daily business, we realised that they could not co-exist, and so we folded after only three weeks due to the strain of it all.

For example, word came to Jimmy one day that his wife was needed urgently in a village about one hour short of Chipata. There was a sick family member desperate for nursing skills and, since we knew Jimmy's wife was a nurse and that the family could not afford an alternative, we could not refuse our brother the fuel he needed for the Bush Baby to carry him there and back.

Then there was the Major from ZAF who came by one evening and asked for some fuel so he could visit his girlfriend in Lusaka. Now it was impossible to refuse him for several reasons. Firstly, he was our friend who had shared many hours, beers and spliffs with us. Secondly, whenever we had any trouble with the law, it was the Major who had our backs. And thirdly, it was the Major who ensured that immigration never asked to see my long-overdue passport that had no work permit.

And then there were the funerals, which we – the young men of The Valley, who many looked up to – were always expected to attend. Each funeral home needed ample wood to keep the fire going throughout the night and that responsibility somehow fell on us. We were required to get into the forest to collect the dead wood, before transporting it all back to the funeral home, where we would start the fire and keep it going until all the wailing was over.

Our fuel was in constant demand and our business could not sustain itself, as the needs of the community far outweighed our desire for profit. Soon after beginning, we started eating into our capital, which forced us to pull the plug on the business and go back to brainstorming.

Ultimately, we made the decision to leave The Valley, because I was too well known and my heart was too soft for profitable gain.

There was simply too much Ubuntu for *muzungu* to succeed.

My life continued to move further away from the Path I was first called to walk, and there were some painful lessons up ahead, just waiting for me to discover.

Capitalism has destroyed our belief in any effective power but that of self-interest backed by force.

- George Bernard Shaw

10

Capitalist

The Lobengula and I travelled six hours south to Chipata on the back of a truck, and then we jumped into a 14-seater minibus filled with 18 people, their *katundu* and a few chickens, to drive west. About two hours into that drive, our minibus slowed down, rode over a speed hump and, as I looked out the window, I saw a sign that read Katete.

I could see the exit from the town as soon as we entered (it was that small), and the road we were on was the only road.

The savannah landscape that surrounded us on either side for the most part of the drive suddenly disappeared and was replaced by a canvas of orange dust. About 20 metres back from the road were scatterings of simple structures similar in size to the shoebox buildings in The Valley. Picture the scene of a small town out of a classic Western movie. Now take away the horses, change the people to Africans, and re-shape the buildings so that they represent what you might find in a South African township.

That's what Katete felt like to me.

Our minibus stopped halfway through town by a shaded area under a few large trees on the left of the road. We exited and The Lobengula took me by the hand and led me straight into Kings, the local nightclub (glorified shebeen) and introduced me to *The Sorcerers*: The Boss; Uncle Den; Junior Mafia; Vampire and the Small-Boy-With-Big-Piston.

The Boss was a tall, coloured man (mixed race); humble and mathematically sharp. He owned Kings, a hardware store and handled the finances for Libean, a family-owned construction business. He was the youngest son of The Family – the Methusalem Phiris – a most highly respected and influential family in Katete who adopted me as their own from day one.

Uncle Den – The Boss' elder brother and the head of operations for Libean – was a big, stocky, spectacled man with a ton of energy, a great

243

dance step and an infectious laugh.

Junior Mafia was a shifty little coloured fellow, slight in stature, with an air of mischievousness all about him. He was also The Boss' right-hand man.

And The Vampire and Small-Boy-With-Big-Piston were two playful young men with a weakness for both beer and the ladies. The Small Boy came from a respected family that ran an agriculture shop, while The Vampire ran his own little cartel amongst the bus drivers and luggage boys.

The Sorcerers were to me, in Katete, what Maison and Rasta were, in The Valley, and as soon as The Lobengula introduced me, they ensured that my right hand never lacked a Mosi.

I spent my early days just hanging out and learning the way of the people, trying to understand how it all worked in relation to the life I had grown accustomed to in The Valley. And there was a lot to learn, a lot of mind-shifting. Katete, though still a rural part of Africa, surrounded by farms, was a town that had sprung up; built by, sustained by and focused on money.

Muzungu.

The spirit of Ubuntu was still very much alive and evident in the relationships and openness of every home, but was not the prevalent mind-set that I had experienced in The Valley. There was a little more urgency to each day, a little more pressure, a little more fear of scarcity and, therefore competition. Daily conversation shifted from the Earth, people and the essence of life, to money; how to find more and how to spend more.

On the one hand, I felt a sense of loss as my memory of the beautiful life in The Valley drifted further into the recesses of my mind. But on the other hand, *muzungu* in me grew steadily excited at the prospect of profit, accumulation and the building of my own empire.

But it was a gradual shift, one that I was not aware of until it was too late.

I've always dreamed of owning a nightclub of my own, and with my background in bars and restaurants, I felt most useful spending my time at Kings. I assisted with DJ-ing, helped introduce a stock control system and started up a Midnight Munchies takeaway section (bite-sized sausage, beef and chicken, flavoured with cheap seasoning, roasted on an open fire in a drum) that boosted business and created a vibe. Of course, free access to a continuously stocked chest freezer of Mosi wasn't a bad perk. It felt good to help – like when I was with Maison, or when I initially began at Mulonga – and I wanted to honour the call of my heart and the spirit of Ubuntu in my new space, by taking ownership of nothing, but simply helping already established businesses to grow past sustenance and into profit. As my mind wandered down the *muzungu* path, however, and saw the potential of it, I slowly allowed my thinking to drift down dangerous paths.

You see, as my days passed in Katete, I found myself missing The Valley more and more, specifically, Mulonga. There was something about the place and my experience there that resonated deep within me. As much as I loved the simple life of the villages, I was aware that it could never remain there, because evolution is a natural process. I was also aware that I would never be fulfilled living in such a rural and detached society, because I had been exposed to so much more throughout my life.

But Mulonga was something different. It is where my mind opened to the possibility that we could truly live in a co-inhabited Africa, where each culture contributed their skills as a gift to the continent, for the sake of the continent, empowering each other along the Way. And the more I sat in Katete and pondered it all, the more my mind began to dream.

I'm quite pissed off that the Mulonga thing didn't work out. I think there was great opportunity there. And that's the weird thing, because I just can't shake the thought from my mind. I keep thinking about the beauty of the place, the nature, the people, the lifestyle. It is the closest to paradise that I have ever been, and there's no way I can ignore that.

I mean, imagine if we could reach a place where the community actually owned their own land, rather than worked on it as an employee of a foreign investor.

What would that look like?

What would it look like if we – the western folk with significantly advanced education –

*partnered with these communities to share
knowledge and skills with them so that they
could make well informed decisions for
the development and growth of their own
community?*

*What would it look like if we shook off the
mentality of ownership from our thinking; if
we, instead, nurtured a mentality of support
… partnership … like a marriage?*

*Wouldn't it be a wonderful thing for visitors to
the continent to stay in and experience the
authentic African culture of a real community;
to sleep in the homes that the people sleep
in; to eat the meals that the people eat; to
hear the stories that have been told around
the fires since the beginning of time, and
which have significantly contributed to the
evolution of the continent; to go on nature
walks and game drives etc. that have been
designed and are led by the very community
that has inhabited the land since the land
was inhabited by humans?*

*I mean, the youth out in The Valley dream
of getting a job on a lodge, that's like the Big*

Dream. That's their imagination of freedom. But imagine if we could plant educational centres for the youth, to equip them with the knowledge and skills they need to develop their own businesses to serve the needs of visitors to the continent?

I want to be a part of this.

I believe that we are moving in this direction.

I need to make some changes and get myself aligned.

The intention, I think, was honourable. All that remained to be seen was whether I could pursue it with a heart of Ubuntu, or whether I would succumb to the lure of *muzungu*.

When one of The Family's trucks broke down and The Boss decided to travel to Johannesburg for spares, I jumped at the opportunity to ride with him. From Johannesburg, I proceeded to Cape Town and worked a few months during tourist season at Panama Jack's Taverna (the best seafood experience you will have in South Africa. Seriously. Just ask for Brian or Liat and tell them I sent you) in the Table Bay Harbour to raise capital to start a business venture with my dearest friend, The Lobengula.

The funniest thing just happened. I arrive home with The Boss and surprise the bejesus out of Mum and – after she gets over the shock of my arrival, my slightly wilder look and very musky scent – she says to me, "Boy, what have you been doing ... you've gone fat! You look good." Mum never misses a thing like that. But that's the wild and crazy thing, because I have been away from home for well over a year and for most of that time I have been living without a single kwacha to my name. I have simply been carried along by the spirit of Ubuntu and the call of my heart. And now I am fatter, better looking and healthier than when I left!

Being in Cape Town, working for money, far away from the life I discovered along the Path of Real Africa, and deep within the western culture and the English language was tough. Things moved fast, people seemed far more superficial in the way they related to each other, conversations were quick and fleeting, and there was a lot of noise

– vehicles, radios, television sets, newspapers, shopping malls and advertising billboards. I really struggled and hated the person that I became in the environment.

But it was for a greater cause, a sacrifice I needed to make for the sake of the bigger picture, so I did it and – in March 2004 – I returned to Katete.

It is a law in Japan that after a certain period of time, it becomes illegal to have a car on the road, and so Japan collects these second-hand cars and ships them off to Durban, where young men and women from across Southern, Eastern and Central Africa travel to buy and transport them back to their nation to sell for profit.

This was a hobby business for The Boss, a way in which he earned his pocket money, and over many conversations he taught me all the intricacies. I learned where to source quality cars, the make that was in demand, the price that the Muslim businessmen asked, the price that The Boss ended up paying, the paperwork that needed to be completed, and also how to proceed without trouble across the borders.

During my time away, The Lobengula busied himself by assessing potential business opportunities that I could invest into. He was diligent in his calculations, and a meticulously disciplined man who was not troubled at sacrificing his own comfort for the sake of the business. So, upon my return, when he made his presentation, I paid attention.

He knew of my desire to establish a community-owned campsite in The Valley, and he knew that this would not be a cheap exercise. So he explained how we needed to align ourselves so that we could eventually move into the business of trading groundnuts. This was what the Muslims were doing – in truckloads – and what was making them extremely wealthy. All that was required was to raise the capital for it, and that process is what he investigated while I was out with The Boss.

He explained how the taxi industry was the next boom phase in Katete's growth, suggested that we buy a Corolla and begin operating, and offered himself to be the tireless taxi driver who demanded no wage.

It all made sense to me, and I decided to go ahead.

The Lobengula and I boarded the suicidal buses that travel the African roads, and made our way to Durban. We took the 30-hour ride to Johannesburg, switched buses at Park Station and continued another eight hours south until we reached the south coast, where we went directly to the beach.

It was his first trip to South Africa and marked the first time he ever saw the ocean. I'll never forget that moment as he stared in awe at the majestic beauty that I take for granted, how cautiously and respectfully he approached the water that I have run fearlessly into since childhood, and the radiant change that came over his face after the whole experience, as if he had had an encounter with God himself. Herself. Itself.

After the beach, we moved directly to the warehouse The Boss had advised us to visit. Within a day we found the Corolla we were looking for, bought it for cash and began our way back to Zambia.

It was a long trip and I was eager to get through it quickly, so I took the wheel, put on the music and engaged racing mode. Just after Masvingo – not far past the Beitbridge border into Zimbabwe – my reckless cornering, together with the cheap retread tyres the vehicle came with and the rough nature of Zimbabwean tarmac earned us a flat tyre. It was only then – at around 10pm on the side of an unlit road, in the middle of obscurity – as we tried to change our tyre under the light of our cell phones that we found out our spare was one of those thin biscuit tyres that only allowed us to travel a maximum of 60 kilometres per hour.

When you are trying to cover around 3000 kilometres in a single trip, such an inconvenience becomes a boulder around the neck. I didn't have the patience nor the discipline, so I shifted to the passenger seat and let my stalwart friend continue.

We travelled from Masvingo up to Harare, a wrong turn there took us about an hour off track to Mutare, where we had to double back for another wasted hour before taking the correct road that led us into Mozambique at the Nyamapanda border. We continued up through the Tete region until we finally crossed into Zambia at a border post that does not exist in Google Maps, and made our way to Katete, to begin our new business venture.

But things did not go according to plan and it wasn't long before we found ourselves in a similar position to our unsuccessful petrol business.

Whenever the Big Man – head of The Family – needed a ride from the farm and into town, The Lobengula was summoned.

Whenever there was a funeral and the grieving family members needed transport, The Lobengula was summoned.

And this happened more often than not.

When Mr Gilbert, the eldest of The Family's brothers needed a ride, The Lobengula was summoned.

When *aMai* (mother of The Family) needed to transport some goods – either to or from her little shop – The Lobengula was summoned.

And it's not like it was a bad thing or against our wishes, because that's not the case. It was an honour to be in a position where such requests were made of us, and we were truly grateful for it all. This was family, and healthy family is the very fabric of a healthy community.

Ubuntu.

Regardless, even though we did not accumulate profit at the rate we had originally hoped for, we did still accumulate profit and the plan remained in place, only with target dates shifted. To compensate for this, I decided to host Katete's Big Braai Party.

Somehow my love for food and music earned me the reputation of being both the best chef in town and the most favoured DJ, so when the posters went up advertising the Party of the Year with Zulu as the main event, the response was staggering.

The stage was set for a weekend of serious partying that promised considerable profit to The Lobengula, me and The Boss. I became so inspired, motivated and involved that I threw myself into the preparations with every bit of energy that I had.

We needed a fence around the property so that we could control the entrance to take fees. The Boss sourced the poles, wire and canvas, and I joined the team of men that constructed it.

One of the speakers had some distortion that was

not up to my satisfaction, so I opened it up, found the problem, travelled to Chipata to buy the parts and came back to fix it. I also decided that we needed a wider variety of music, so I travelled to Lusaka to hear what was playing in the clubs of the 'big city', contacted some DJs and pirated a good selection.

I bought, cleaned, cut, spiced and marinated around 20 chickens and 15 kilograms of beef; I made the coleslaw and the spicy tomato chutney to go with it all; I was everywhere at once, involved in everything.

But *muzungu's* single-minded approach to life narrowed my vision and I failed to see the irregularities that led to my demise.

Being so caught up in my pursuit for financial gain, I did not notice how, each day at roughly the same time, The Lobengula would make a trip to the nearby Secondary School. I also failed to notice how all The Sorcerers, except The Boss, would disappear from sight together with him. And though I should have known better, I did not consider the power of penis at the time of a party.

Katete is a town full of *mahule*: women who –
through their desire for the alluring objects that
only money can buy – have given themselves
over to the dark side of their sexuality. This meant
that Katete was not the ideal town for a young
man to find his mate, because women with morals
were noticeably absent. Now, for most of the men
of Katete, this was not a problem, because men
with morals were equally absent.

But for my merry little band – The Sorcerers – this
posed a problem.

They did not want *mahule*, they wanted girls of
purity and innocence, who they could love and
nurture into womanhood. But these girls were
kept safely away from the town, in the hostels of
Katete Secondary School – the school that our
taxi visited more and more frequently as the days
to our Big Party grew closer.

Completely unaware of the decrease in labour
force for the event, I continued to push myself to
make sure that we delivered what was expected.
The result, however, was that I weakened my
usually tenacious immune system, which opened
the door for malaria, just two days before the

function. In a part of the world where medication is scarce, where quinine tablets are the most accessible treatment for a disease that has long since become quinine-resistant, the only real option for a stubborn man like myself was to dig deep and push through.

And so I did just that, working myself into exhaustion to organise the party of the year.

The food, once thrown on the fire to roast, carried a tantalising flavour into the air that drew in the crowds. The beer was plentiful, the ladies were dressed for sex and the music absolutely turned the dance floor upside down.

Sales sky-rocketed, the money rolled in, success was achieved and then I collapsed, exhausted, burnt-out and almost destroyed by Africa's killer disease that takes a life every 60 seconds.

Bed-ridden and in the throes of malarial hell, I experienced the warm love of my adopted family. Members visited me each day to ensure that I had a steady supply of food, tea and warm water for baths. And between the disease and the caring hospitality of The Family, I did not notice the undercurrent of something suspicious amongst The Sorcerers. It was only when I finally emerged from the room to soak up some sunshine in my second week of recovery that I saw the Corolla – *my* Corolla – parked outside with its back window smashed to pieces.

The story goes like this...

During the days preceding the Big Party, The Sorcerers successfully found their suitable mates, and had made the required plans to collect them on the night of the function. Their idea was to sneak the girls out of school and into town to rejoice with them in drunken revelry, with the clear intention of sleeping with them at some stage. What The Sorcerers did not know was that while they were formulating their plans, the high school boys had caught wind of it and had set into motion their own intended retaliation.

So on the night of the party, while I was under the chains of malaria and slaving away to make up for the financial shortfall we were experiencing with the taxi business, The Lobengula and The Sorcerers – under the mixed influence of alcohol and penis – decided to fulfil their mission and headed off to school to collect their ladies. It was a resounding success and there was much celebration in the Corolla as The Lobengula navigated his way out of the school yard. The Sorcerers turned on the music, opened the wine for the ladies and settled back for a night fit for kings.

Then came the ambush.

The high school boys placed a spotter at the school's entrance and, as soon as the Corolla arrived, he sent out the call to his peers. While The Sorcerers were schmoozing their ladies, the high school ambush team darted to the exit gate, threw a branch across the road, and hid themselves in the thicket. The Lobengula reached the exit, cursed the poor school maintenance that allowed for branches to be left lying idle on the road, and stopped the car to remove it. As soon as he did, the ambush team jumped out of the bush and began hurling bricks at our taxi. One bounced off the roof, another bounced off the driver's door, and the third went straight through the rear window.

This was the story I found myself in the middle

of, as I emerged from 10 days of malaria-induced fever.

To replace the window would have cost around half a million kwacha and flattened all our savings. The other alternative was to get *nkongole* (credit from a local businessman), but The Lobengula and I had drawn a line in the sand at the very beginning to say that we would never attempt to grow our business by going into debt. In my disgust, I ordered him to sell the car and wait for me, while I returned to Cape Town's Panama Jacks to raise the capital we needed to begin wholesaling groundnuts.

Four months later, I returned to Katete and found things slightly different from what we had originally planned.

The Lobengula was sitting in the office of a rural business centre that he had started, with two young girls under his employ. While I was away, he decided that it was a wiser decision to invest the cash into a shop rather than to risk it in groundnuts. And so he opened up Katete's first business centre, which was two PC's and a photocopier/printer, with an incredibly slow dial-up internet connection.

In hindsight, it was a responsible decision, but in my youthfulness and, with *muzungu* fully in control of my thinking, I felt that I needed to move faster.

I walked over to Kings and went straight to the fridge for a Mosi.

But the fridge was empty.

I walked across the road to Drums, our competitor, but he also had no stock, and complained bitterly about how The Boss was intentionally keeping the container supply low so that Kings would be the only liquor outlet with beer on the weekend.

I knew this was not true and that Junior Mafia had probably made a bad deal, which resulted in the shambles.

I crossed back over the road to the hardware shop and made a proposal to The Boss to invest all my money into the container.

It was a good move.

A perpetually full beer container meant that everyone from Katete to Petauke could rely on getting drunk each weekend. And in a part of the world where beer and *mahule* ruled, that was very important. What it also meant was that every business owner running a liquor outlet within a 100-kilometre radius would stop badmouthing The Boss and The Family, accusing them of being a cartel. And considering the good name that The Family upheld, this was another extremely important mess to fix up.

Over and above those two good points, my investment also meant that I would own the stock, and that made me a powerful player in the town of Katete. This was the pinnacle that *muzungu* had urged me to reach, and what should have followed was years of easy living.

But it didn't work out that way.

Junior Mafia was in charge of operations at the container, and he did not inherit that name without reason. A slightly built, boyish-looking coloured chap with an impish nature, Junior Mafia was a little tyrant, a wheeler dealer. Being The Boss's head of operations gave him direct access to many things, and he spent most of his time using money that came into the container to finance his own side business deals. He would pocket the profit and then return the money to the container before depositing the weekly sales into the bank account.

It was a good system that only The Sorcerers knew about.

He smuggled booze from Mozambique into Zambia, and traded in small amounts of maize, sunflower oil, petrol, groundnuts and anything else that would generate a quick profit for his own pocket.

He was the master, he was Junior Mafia.

But he lived a high life and his girlfriend was high maintenance, and a gradual increase in pressure forced him to take some risks that did not pay. And so as The Boss's stock in the container steadily reduced, Junior Mafia started using my funds, which I became aware of only on the day I decided to make a withdrawal.

After two weeks with Junior Mafia being invisible, running up and down trying to make collections to satisfy my demand, I realised that I was in a sinking ship. Katete was a town that had only recently been introduced to money, and most of the people who had access to it, had no education about it. The result was a community that was being taken over by the hunger. Brother was cheating brother, sister was seducing friend, husband was lying to wife and children … and all of this because the hunger for money had grown greater than the values the community was built upon.

Muzungu.

It was a mess, and as long as I remained there, I began to believe that I would fail. Even my closest friend, The Lobengula used to joke:

"Man, this place is poison. I am telling you, even if Jesus came to spend some time here, he would either run away or get drunk and end up sleeping with some *mahule* ... and Bill Gates, he would walk back home with no shoes on his feet, naked and destroyed!"

We laughed at this every time, and we still laugh about it today, mostly because of its truth.

Desperate for my own financial success, I shifted my attention and began asking a new set of

267

questions, which led to a new set of options. As I followed these conversations, I was introduced to The Bull, and through him, I learned about the motor vehicle spare parts trade.

The Bull was a short, fat and uncomfortable-looking man from the Choma region of Southern Zambia. A sweet-talker and con-artist, the Bull had been involved in cross-border business for some time and had learned the intricacies of moving goods without attracting large customs and duties charges. In fact, he was well renowned.

A man not to be trusted with even one kwacha, The Bull was good at what he did. And when he explained to me how the parts that were being supplied into Zambia all came from South Africa, it was an opportunity I could not resist. I teamed up with him and got myself into the spares game.

Our business grew rapidly and catapulted me up the ranks into the category of *Big Bwana* (big boss). We travelled by bus to South Africa, bought approximately a ton of spares and a People magazine, loaded these back onto the bus and returned to Zambia about once every month. Law required us to pay approximately 65 per cent tax to the government for every trip we made, which was ludicrous and could never allow for the retailers in Zambia to sell at a price that was affordable for the people, so a system was devised to bypass this.

Transporting our goods with a local passenger bus meant that all official documentation could be changed, as opposed to using a transport company who would require the original invoices. With The Bull's system, the original invoices never made it out of South Africa. After collecting all our goods from our suppliers, we then spent hours creating invoices of our own that reduced the cost of goods by approximately 90 per cent.

So a part that cost us R500 was re-invoiced to cost R50. These doctored invoices were the ones we presented to customs officials at the Zambian border, and these are what we were taxed on. What was even more ingenious on the part of The Bull is that he had figured out how, by using public transport instead of a dedicated transport company to carry our stock, we gave the impression of being poor men struggling to eke out a living, as opposed to successful businessmen who could afford our expenses. Such a scenario, together with The Bull's well-practised look of sorrow, attracted mercy at the border and opened the door for negotiations.

And The Bull was a master negotiator (con man).

The trips to Chirundu border were familiar to me; they were no different from the first trip I made when I began my Journey back in 2002. Only in these last days, I was one of those people who were carrying giant loads of *katundu* with me.

I was usually quiet around the border, keeping myself out of sight. The Bull explained how, if I was seen with the *katundu*, the customs officials would quickly deduce that they were able to get larger bribes and this would damage our negotiating power. So upon arrival, The Bull and I split up. I'd visit the rastaman, take a walk to a nearby liquor outlet, chill out, sip on Mosi and mingle about like a tourist while The Bull walked back and forth in his lagging gait, sweating profusely as he negotiated our way through.

But there was one time when I hung around to watch, and what I learned truly impressed me.

It started with a greeting:

"*Bwanji aMdala?*" (How are you, Big Man?)

This was then followed by a set of more personal questions.

"*Kunyumba bwanji?*" (How are things at home?)

"*aMwana bwanji?*" (How is your child?)

"*aMai bwanji?*" (How is the mother of your child?)

"*Bwanji kunchito?*" (How are things at work?)

These were the disarming questions that levelled the playing field and opened the door for negotiations.

"*Ndo'kupya lelo.*" (Man, it is hot today)

"*Mufuna drink?*" (Would you like a cool drink?)

"*Mwana, bwelesa madrinks uwiri. Tamanga!*" (Boy, bring two drinks. Hurry!)

The nearest youngster dashed off and returned with two bottled cool drinks, The Bull handed over some cash and relaxed in the knowledge that he had made it past the first wall of government defence.

From here, he was in his element.

As The Bull and the customs officer shared their drink together, light conversation continued, with The Bull making a special effort to crack jokes that allowed him to hold the officer's hand or pat him on the shoulder, as they both laughed.

During this interchange, all defences crumbled, and The Bull established a friendship.

I watched on with eager anticipation and noticed much laughter and light-heartedness, during which time the Bull handed over a *People* magazine to the government official. What nobody saw was that while they were talking and laughing, The Bull was also negotiating. He was given an amount from the official that he either accepted or refused.

When he refused, the negotiations continued, when he accepted, he handed over the magazine. Somewhere in there were some US dollars, which the customs official removed before handing the magazine back to him. From there, The Bull moved back to our *katundu* and the customs official walked over to one of his juniors to exchange a few short words.

This procedure continued for about three hours every trip, and it was no easy task, because everyone needed their share. Customs, immigration and police were all as important as luggage boys, foreign exchange traders and security guards; every one of them played a vital role in helping the poor, average Zambian who was being suffocated by oppressive government policies. And each of us simple traders owed a lot to them for their service. In order to express that, it was necessary to show appreciation, and appreciation could be costly. (in some countries, appreciation is considered as bribery, but we did not believe in bribery. We only believed in showing appreciation to those who assisted us along the way. Similar to the Christmas gifts that customers get from their suppliers every year, in more developed nations)

Too little appreciation, and the path through Chirundu would be slightly tighter to walk the next time we passed by; too much appreciation, and not only would we lower our profits, but we would also raise the bar and make it more difficult for every future trader.

Managing appreciation was a vital part in the chess game that is the Chirundu border, but The Bull was a grandmaster.

The guy worked magic.

He had a round head with fat creases at the back, no neck and a child-like grin that portrayed a gentle and shy little boy. Women felt safe around him and he was able to work his charm and keep our appreciation well below average. He was renowned for this and reduced our expenses by a significant amount.

The Bull's border tactics, together with my South African citizenship that allowed me to source products from a variety of places at a fraction of the cost, expanded our business rapidly.

We operated in a four-week cycle:

As soon as we arrived in Lusaka from the border, we offloaded our *katundu* into The Bulls' humble, two-bedroom home that could barely sustain the people living there without our ton of boxes filling up every empty space. Within the first week we made all our phone calls to customers, informing them that their goods had arrived. We then told them what day to expect delivery and to ensure that payment was waiting for us to collect upon our arrival. As soon as that was done, we loaded our *katundu* onto buses and began the two-week trip that covered approximately 6000 kilometres.

From Lusaka we went north, stopping at Kapiri Mposhi, Kabwe, Ndola, Kitwe, Luanshya and Chingola. We then headed west to Solwezi before returning to Lusaka, where we'd stop to collect our goods for the Eastern Province section of our business. We'd stop at Nyimba, Petauke, Katete and Chipata, before boarding a Canter to The Valley and then returning to Lusaka.

We delivered the goods and collected our payments in US dollars cash, together with our orders for the following month. As soon as this was done, we boarded the earliest bus for our trip to Johannesburg to repeat the cycle.

It was an exhausting process, but – in *muzungu's* eyes – with all the untaxed cash that flowed through our pockets, it was worth it.

Wherever we went, we sat amongst police chiefs, army majors, commissioners, politicians and other very successful businessmen. I found myself in the midst of discussions around the illegal smuggling of gemstones, ivory and marijuana, amongst others. We ordered whatever we wanted from the menu, drank to our heart's content, and seldom paid for any of it. And that was important, because every official needed to show their appreciation for our business, which financed their children's school fees, their wives' and girlfriends' perfumes and leather jackets, and their own cell phones and fancy watches.

I relocated to Lusaka, formed a company, opened a bank account, rented a house, bought a Nissan Hardbody and set up an office with storage space for our goods, giving us a more professional look that also allowed for swifter service delivery.

The Lobengula moved from Katete to join me and all was well, as financial prosperity surrounded both us and those who associated themselves with us.

It was all good and I was well on my way to realising the dream.

But the truth I neglected to see was that I had stepped far off the Path I had originally started walking, and had long since stopped listening to the call of my heart.

The stars of Real Africa still twinkled, the spirit of Ubuntu still burned in my heart, but *muzungu* in me was so in control that I was oblivious to it all.

And although everything looked good from the outside, within hidden places I could not comprehend, forces of raw carnage were already set in motion to bring me to my knees.

Let go of the idea that your path will get you to your goal. The truth is that with every step you take, you have already arrived.

- Paulo Coelho

11

The Makuti Incident

November 2005, five years after hearing the Voice, and four years after responding.

The Hardbody did a lot of work and it was the heart of our operations, so when its odometer indicated service time, I did not hesitate to take it back to South Africa. Fortunately the trip coincided perfectly with a business need, so there was no wasted time or resources to worry about.

In the world of African trade, I discovered the value of cash. We'd collect it from our customers and carry it across the borders, straight into Johannesburg city centre where a certain Muslim businessman, who sold blankets to the public at wholesale prices, offered the best foreign exchange rate we could find anywhere south of the DRC. At times we would get as much as 5c extra for every rand we bought. Now that seems silly, but when you consider that we were exchanging around US$10000 at a time, that translated into a saving of about R3500, which settled all our travel expenses.

It was good business.

In the few weeks before my departure, The Bull and I managed to collect around US$9000, which we intended using to restock our warehouse. That was a clever little part of our business strategy that pushed us ahead of our competitors, because while they travelled south to collect parts before they could supply their orders, we sneakily cut in and supplied their customers directly from our warehouse in Lusaka. It was a tactic that created quite a bit of animosity, but *muzungu* did not care, because profit was more important than relationships.

On 6 November 2005 I awoke early in the morning, took my bath, ate my breakfast and jumped into the *bakkie* with my backpack, laptop and three Red Bulls, to begin a perfectly ordinary trip that eventually led to extraordinary consequences.

I expected temperatures to easily rise above 40 degrees, so my early start was intended to beat the heat to Chirundu. After that there was no way to escape the scorching stretch to Harare, but I had my Red Bulls and Bob Marley to counter any tiredness that attempted to creep in. I reached the border around 8am, paid my usual gratuities to all and sundry, climbed back into the Hardbody, unbuttoned my shirt, left my seatbelt unbuckled and settled in for the six-hour drive that lay ahead of me.

From here, things get a bit hazy.

I was on a narrow, dual-lane road that carved its way through a sea of khaki sand, scattered with unimpressive trees, many of which were dry and leafless. Above me was a clear blue sky. I remember two white police vans – Toyota Land Cruisers – which I overtook just before a gentle, sweeping left curve that led me into a stretch of road that continued straight until it disappeared into an horizon of shimmering heat.

And then my memory fails me.

Before I left Chirundu, I sent my father a text message to update him on my schedule; I expected to arrive in Harare around midday, Beitbridge border between six and seven that evening, and home around midnight. That bit of communication was usual protocol, because as soon as I entered Zimbabwe, my cell phone coverage ended and there was no way for anyone in the world to know where I was or how I was doing.

Evening came and Dad received no phone call.

But he was not perturbed, since he had monitored me and The Bull for a few months and was well accustomed to African-time, the many things that control its pace, and the countless variables that were in operation along our particular business path. Later that night when he had still received no call, he accepted that I had decided to proceed straight from Beitbridge without phoning and that I was en route home, so he lay himself down to rest with a peaceful mind.

But around seven the following morning when he had still received no communication, he decided to call and check in on me.

At first he got only my voicemail. Then he called Lusaka and got hold of The Lobengula, who only confirmed what Dad already knew – I had crossed over Chirundu around 8am the morning before, and should have been home, ravenously devouring my mother's mutton curry. He then made a call to Foreign Affairs, who transferred him to South Africa's ambassador in Harare, who searched as far as he could, but returned with no useful information. By the time evening came, my mother was convinced that her youngest child was dead, and my father remained silent with nothing more than a fine strand of hope and desperate faith in an unseen God. It was all he had to cling to, so later that night he refused to sleep and chose to bruise his knees as he knelt beside his bed and prayed.

"Philén is alive and needs your help. Go to Zimbabwe."

This is what he heard within himself at some stage during his prayerful pleading. He wanted to believe that it was God ... he so desperately wanted to believe, but he also accepted that without sleep and food, and with a fair amount of anxiety, that he was most likely delusional.

"God, if that is you then give me a sign, a confirmation, something certain, please."

He got off his knees, climbed into bed and finally drifted off to sleep, exhausted.

For 29 years my father had watched me grow. He knew my voice before it was anything comprehensible; when it was merely a mumbling of sounds. He heard me utter my first coherent syllable and watched me develop into a public speaker addressing hundreds of people. So in a dream, when my voice called out to him, he needed no explanation.

"Dad. Dad! Come. I need you here."

He woke Mum, assured her that I was alive and that he needed to get to Zimbabwe to find me. A quick call was made to my favourite aunt, who scrambled and moved mountains to secure tickets for Dad to get there on such short notice. Donnie, a long-time family friend (more like sibling) joined Dad for moral support and, in a flash, they were off on their spur-of-the-moment trip to Zimbabwe, a destination my father had never previously visited.

Immediately upon their arrival in Harare, Dad and Donnie were met by Old-Man Colin – another family friend – and it was Dad who spoke first.

"Donnie, you and I will go south from here to Beitbridge."

"And I'll get on the phone to call every hospital from Chirundu to Harare," Colin added.

They agreed to call each other as soon as anyone heard any news, and then set off on their different missions. Dad and Donnie drove the 600-kilometre stretch from Harare to Beitbridge with a photograph of me, stopping at every hospital, police station and mortuary as they travelled. But for all their efforts, they only managed to find out that nobody knew anything about me. Colin, on the other hand, remained in one spot and phoned every hospital from Chirundu to Harare.

It was a long and futile day, and as each hour passed and the day entered the early stages of evening, hope was very low.

When Dad's phone rang, he answered without much expectation.

"Colin has found the boy," Mum exclaimed. "He's in a hospital!"

We never did find out exactly what happened and my memory has not given me even the slightest hint. But The Lobengula did take a trip back to the scene of it all and spoke to an old man by the roadside, and this is the story as he told it:

"The car was coming behind a truck. Tanzanian. The car came out to pass, but Tanzanian was also turning for the rest-stop. I saw the car hit brakes but his front left catch the back of truck and the car spins and rolls. One, two, and the man flies out of window in front of the car.

He goes high in the air. Like a bird.

And then lands on his back. Like an egg.

We are standing. Watching.

We want to get the man but his car is still rolling towards him.

Three, four.

And then, it's like the hand of God reaches out to catch the car and put it down just next to man."

When The Lobengula tells me this story, he dramatises it the way he recalls, and the part that always gets me is the look on his face at the end of the story. Big, wide eyes of absolute disbelief.

Apparently the local villagers immediately ran to my side to see if they could help. Thankfully the police vans I had overtaken arrived before they attempted to move me, and thankfully Mr Peters – a stranger – arrived in his Pajero before the cops tried loading me into the back of their all-steel-interior van.

I was in a place known as Makuti, which is a few hundred metres past the sign that reads, "You are now entering the middle of nowhere." It is about as remote a place as you can find in the grasslands of sub-Saharan Africa that is still inhabited by humans. Mr Peters loaded me into the back of his Pajero and took me off to the local Makuti clinic where the nurses took one look at me and directed him to Karoi hospital.

And it is in this hospital, after many phone calls, that Colin found me.

Colin phoned Mum, Mum phoned Dad, and Dad phoned Karoi hospital.

"Very bad, sir. Very, very bad. Completely unconscious. Doctor shines light into eyes, but nothing. Completely nothing. Doctor put on drip and says we wait for him to wake up. But we don't think he wakes. Completely unconscious. Nothing. But when old man phones, I go to bed and he opens his eyes and say to me, 'where is the dollars?', then I know that something has happened."

I was unconscious, unable to be awakened, incapable of being able to react with my surroundings, unresponsive to any pain or sound, and my eyes did not react to light. But at the same time as Colin phoned in search of me, at the same time as the joint prayers around the world of our family and friends were offered in terrified hope for a miracle – I woke up without any prompting (please don't ask me to explain this. I am still searching for answers). And when the phone was handed to me by the nurse, and when I heard my Dad's voice, my first words were:

"Dad, where's the dollars? Where am I?"

My father told me not to worry about the money, as he climbed back into the car with Donnie to make his way to me in Karoi.

I don't know how long he was at my side before I opened my eyes, but when I saw him, my question remained.

"Dad! Where's the dollars?"

My father looked at me with a searching gaze, eyes filled with love yet glazed over with an indefinable pain.

"Lie still, boy. Something bad has happened."

"And where's Jean? He was in the car with me, Dad! Where's Jean?"

Jean was The Bull's younger brother, and my father was not aware that he was travelling with me. When he heard my frantic questions and matched this against the nurse's information that the police had been at the hospital and had asked to be notified when I awoke, he decided to follow what seemed like a hot trail. But a call to The Bull back in Zambia set the record straight. Jean was in Lusaka, exactly where he was supposed to be, despite my delusional insistence that he was in the car when I drove it to the hospital parking lot with a few scratches and dents.

Donnie and Dad knew exactly what they needed

to do next. They needed to see the vehicle.

But it was not in the parking lot as they had hoped it would be, so they decided to take a drive back along the road, which they expected me to have used from Chirundu. About 80 kilometres away, they finally found it with a little more than a few scratches and dents. Lying idle on the side of the road, a few metres away from a traffic speed sign that had been uprooted from the ground and smashed like a used toothpick was the remains of the Hardbody. A complete write-off. Windscreen smashed, canopy obliterated and the vehicle's engine so noticeably shifted that there was not enough space in the driver's cockpit for even a child to fit in at a squeeze.

The remnants of the vehicle provided evidence that it was physically impossible for any human being to come out alive, physically impossible for a human being to even manage to come out at all.

As my Dad reached in to the mess to rescue the laptop and some containers of petrol, he pondered that perhaps all was not as it appeared to flow from my tongue, so he and Donnie drove back to

Karoi, continuing their mission to bring clarity to a murky situation.

Upon returning to Karoi, my father decided to visit the police, knowing that they were waiting for me to wake. Only one cop was on duty and he accompanied both Donnie and Dad to the hospital, where he demanded to speak to me, but my father refused. He was happy to let the police officer see me, but not for him to disturb my already disturbed mental state.

When the cop started bullying, ordering that I not leave the country until I faced a court hearing to explain the accident, my father knew that it was time to show some appreciation, which he did before sending the cop on his way to enjoy the weekend.

Dad then asked to see the doctor and requested that I be immediately released into his care, but was refused. He followed that with a phone call and arranged for a South African doctor to issue the same request, which was, thankfully, granted.

Finally I was rolled out in a wheelchair to the parking lot, and then driven away to a motel for the night. The Zimbabwean doctor's report that was handed to us stated that all X-rays were clear and that no serious injury was caused.

The following morning I boarded an aeroplane back to South Africa, where I was booked into Wilgeheuwel private hospital.

Immediately upon arrival, the doctor on duty called for a neurosurgeon and, after running his tests, the specialist responded with words that shook my father's Soul.

"Severe head trauma, multiple skull fractures, a neck fracture, and brain contusions that have created considerable pressure within his skull. Thank God they did not find these results with their tests in Zimbabwe. They would surely have decided to operate, and your boy would probably have died."

Seven years later, as I write this story, my memory still fails me on most issues, but there are a few things, completely random, that I do recall. For example, there was a group of Christian folk, strangers, who surrounded my bed and prayed for me. Apparently I was asleep when they arrived, but at some point during their prayer I smiled and woke up.

There was also a gothic-looking girl named Mandy, who came by and brought me some motoring magazines.

I remember the cheesecake I was served every day and the warm cup of Milo I drank every evening. Wilgeheuwel is still my all-time favourite hospital and, as far as hospitals go, I fully recommend it.

I also remember how my mother would visit each afternoon on her way home from school, each time bringing with her some delicious home-cooked curry.

There was also this one time when I tried climbing down from my bed, needing to pee, but collapsed along the way, and someone had to pick me up.

I remember that. It was very humbling.

And then I remember Dad who sat by my bedside and never seemed to leave.

I honestly do not remember much else.

Three weeks passed, apparently more torturous for my family than for me, as they dealt with my many pleas for morphine, together with countless threats of how I would leopard-crawl down the passage and out the window as soon as they were out of sight. But eventually, after the madness settled, I found myself walking to the neurosurgeon's room, with my mother by my side. I didn't fall, so I figured I was healed and that my release was a mere formality. My spirits were high as I walked into his office and took my seat in front of him.

"Are you a praying man?" the specialist questioned. Not quite the words anyone wants to hear from their neurosurgeon.

I nodded, remembering how I had been raised with the habit; that I had once believed in and practised it, but not for the past few years.

The doctor leaned back in his chair with a look on his face that only a doctor who is about to deliver some bad news can wear.

"The truth is – medically – there is nothing we can do." He turned to address my mother and continued.

"No surgery will heal what has been damaged.

His frontal lobe, together with crucial neural pathways, has been irreparably scarred. I truly do suggest you pray."

At first I stared blankly at the man. Then I stared right through him, his chair and the walls that surrounded us. I was lost, gazing into a terrifyingly dark future when Mum took my hand and led me away.

No words were said.

We reached home and I walked directly to my room, dropped to my knees and cried the softest, most sincere prayer I have ever offered.

November 2005.

You have to leave the city of your comfort and go into the wilderness of your intuition. What you'll discover will be wonderful. What you'll discover is yourself.

- Alan Alda

12

There Is No Finish Line

March 2008.

I started, lost.

Who am I?

Why am I here?

What's the point?

As I questioned, I searched. Within me and outside of me.

And as I searched, I discovered.

Many things.

Some I enjoyed, others were pretty difficult to face up to, but it was all part of the Journey.

I held this belief in my heart that up ahead was a place that made me very happy, a space where I find my freedom and live in it. And this belief is what carried me through every day. No matter what happened, I somehow managed to convince myself that it was all part of a greater plan, and that plan was good. So I accepted all of it with gratitude, and walked through to the day's end ... every day, with eager anticipation of the adventure that lay ahead.

But now I'm here ... and it's all a little confusing ...

I was in my tent, in my parent's garden. I needed desperately to reconnect with my Soul, to hear the Voice, to know that I was alive ... not just living.

I couldn't find a Table Mountain in Johannesburg, so the next best option my brain came up with was to pitch tent in the garden.

And that's what I did.

My mother's garden is a little piece of paradise, with flowers and trees and the insects they attract; with birds and the neighbour's cats that love to hunt them; with butterflies and dragonflies, ladybirds and cicadas. It is truly a sacred space filled with life, crafted by Love.

I disconnected from technological civilisation and took my single gas cooker, a pot, Swiss army knife and wooden spoon, and packed them neatly next to my journal and stack of books (the Bible, Baghavad Gita, Awakening of Intelligence, Gospel of Buddha and Celestine Prophecy are all books that have played a major role in my Journey). And then I withdrew from the world, with my guitar, for an indefinite period of time.

I had questions.

I needed answers.

And I was not interested in timelines.

If it took two minutes for me to receive what I was searching for, then so be it.

If it took 40 years, then so be it.

As is the pattern in our family, Mum thought that I was mad and Dad had to make peace with that, loving and respecting his wife, yet allowing his son to be.

The time that followed my release from hospital was difficult for me to understand. I knew that I was not well, because the doctors had all made that very clear. I also didn't feel 100%, and the constant look of concern on both mother and father's faces, and the way they tip-toed around me was something I could not ignore either.

At the same time however, I was 29 years young and on a Journey that was being led by a Voice within me that existed beyond space and time, which I believed was from God herself/himself/itself. Failure – in my corrupt little mind – was not possible. That being said, I was caught in a space between two conflicting realities, and I struggled to find my truth in it.

Was my Journey over, because of the injuries I had sustained?

Or was my Journey still well on track, just with a little twist … a detour that my mind could not comprehend, but which was all good?

I chose to believe the latter and stayed in business with my father, mindful of the financial loss we had suffered and which needed recovering. But as I waded through my days, I grew more aware of what was happening within me.

I wasn't as sharp as I remembered myself to be. I wanted to believe that I was, and I placed myself in situations to prove it, but it didn't work out. I struggled with basic spreadsheets, I failed to remember orders that I had placed, I miscalculated formulae, forgot my keys countless times, and the list goes on.

My friend would call me from a phone booth in London, and speak to me for hours, only to receive a frantic text message the next day asking her where she's been and why hasn't she called because I missed her.

Then there were days where I would sit on the edge of the bath tub with a towel around my waist, for ridiculous lengths of time, not being able to comprehend where I was or what I was supposed to be doing.

When I punched a hole through the study door, pushed my mother up against the wall, and held a knife to my father, my neurologist decided to give me some medication. He explained how there was no cure for my condition, but how the medication would make me more manageable.

Anti-depressants. Urgh! They felt like really cheap ecstasy pills and had a similar 'come down' effect that left me craving my next 'hit'. And somewhere in that moment of my life, I discovered how broken I was and how desperately I needed rescuing, if the Journey was to continue to a good end.

Now, I walked away from the church 12 years earlier. I never really believed in it all, but I had followed along like good children do, trying to please all those around me. As soon as I completed school, though, and went away for my gap year, I turned my back on the religious institution that I had found to be a fountain of hypocrisy, judgment and self-serving philosophies that promoted one culture above all others.

My mother and father however, remained faithful to the path they had chosen and – during my post-Makuti time – they were involved in the planting of a new church in the west of Johannesburg. Taking advantage of my broken mental state, Dad invited me to this church one Sunday, and being as desperate as I was, I did not argue. Although, between you and me, I did have it in my mind that I would go along only so that I would have reason enough to decline the invitation the following week.

I can't tell you much about that church service. I don't remember the dude who spoke, or what he spoke about. But I do remember that there were only like 16 people in a little room that was part of a thatched restaurant adjacent to a river. That was cool. It felt homely.

But the thing that really got my attention was the man who greeted me when I arrived. He was a guy known as Frodo; a fairly respectable man in the corporate world, in his early forties, with hair down to his shoulders. And as soon as he saw me, he gave me the warmest and most memorable hug, the kind that you would expect to get from Winnie the Pooh. And it is that hug that disarmed me and led me back the next week.

Over time, I grew close to Frodo and a solid trust formed between us, mainly because he had a past more messed up than mine, so I could relate to him. He was real. So one day when he spoke to me about a 'church where crazy stuff happens', I was intrigued and decided to follow the trail.

Out in Northcliff was a place known as Solid Rock, and they called themselves 'the church of miracles'. Frodo told me how he had been there before and had seen some pretty incredible healing take place. Blind people got their sight back, lame people walked etc. It sounded so ridiculous that I couldn't refuse. And since I was not allowed to drive, in my condition, I went along with my Dad. Somehow, I guess that was a good thing, because – at least – there is a credible witness to the very abridged version of the story I am about to tell …

The pastor guy was off the streets of Hillbrow, and his speech was quite free and rough, which I appreciated because it made him more human and easier to relate to. Anyway, while he was standing up there and doing his thing, he suddenly turned directly to me.

"What's wrong with you, bru? You look pretty messed up."

I kinda mumbled something, and then he walked over to me to continue the conversation.

"You are a mighty warrior." he said, "and you can't do what God wants you to do, if you're all messed up like this. You need to receive your healing."

I listened to the man, but didn't really follow him.

He asked a few questions, I answered some, my Dad answered others, and then he prayed for me. And that was that.

Now, I've already mentioned this, but I will say it again. I was seriously messed up. My brain injuries and the state of my life was in such dire need of a miracle that I gravitated, without thought, to wherever I was led. Honestly, if it so happened that someone came along and promised me healing, if I went with them to Kathmandu to perform oral sex on an hermaphrodite donkey, I would probably have gone without batting an eyelid.

Thankfully, nobody came with such an offer.

Anyway, my point is that I had absolutely no clue about what was going on. On the one hand, it all sounded absolutely mental. But then, on the other hand, the best neurosurgeons, neurologists and neuropsychologists had all been unanimous in their verdict that there was no medical solution for my injuries.

Honestly, what choice did I have?

So, like an innocent child, I believed what the

pastor said about this fellow Jesus and the healing power that is found in him, and went back, with my father, the next week.

And the next.

And the next.

Until the day came for a specific healing service, for which I had generated enough ignorant hope.

Now I can't explain much about much, so please don't ask me to. All I can do is tell the story, as it happened … although it is heavily abridged, because I don't feel the details are important.

What I do know was important, was that there was a lot of prayer (again, I will not go into definitions of a god that was prayed to, because I believe that such definitions miss the point quite drastically). And at some stage in it all, my legs went weak and I slowly drifted away. It literally felt as if I was being swallowed by a giant ball of light. I felt very safe and comfortable, and can remember being placed gently on the floor.

While I lay there, it felt as if a million little ants were crawling around under the skin of my face, and in my skull. That might sound terrifying to you, but I remember it being quite ticklish, and I think I might have smiled, although I can't be sure, because I could not see myself.

I don't know how long I was on the floor, you will need to ask my Dad about this, but when I eventually opened my eyes, I do know that I was smiling. I jumped up to my feet, looked my father square in the eyes and declared:

"Dad, I'm healed."

I don't know what my father thought, but we walked together to the car, with me not needing any assistance to keep my balance, and with a bounce in my step that I had long forgotten. We reached home, I dished myself a plate of curry and rice, and then threw my medication in the bin.

The following morning, I awoke to find mother all packed and ready to take me to the neurologist. She was a good Christian and all, but the hole in the door as she walked down the passage was a very real reminder of what could happen when I was not taking my happy pills.

The neurologist did his tests and ran the necessary scans, the neuropsychologist did his thing, and both of them returned to my mother with the same conclusion:

"You have a miracle child."

And that was it. I was healed.

Not completely, though, because to this day, I still have absolutely no sense of smell. Not a thing. And that's my reminder … I just don't know of what. Maybe it's to remind me of my humanity. Maybe it's to keep me striving, pushing, pursuing the seemingly impossible, so that I can overcome mental barriers that were planted within me before my birth by a society that seems to thrive on fear and self-sabotage.

Time will tell.

Now, there are many different opinions and philosophies around what I experienced.

Each religious group has their belief.

Within each group, there are different sects, denominations etc., who all have differing perspectives from each other.

Then there are all those who do not belong to any religious group, and they each have their own opinions.

There are the atheists, who claim they don't believe in god or God. This always amuses me, because as soon as you say that you don't believe in something, you speak that thing into existence. Anyway, these dear brothers and sisters of mine have an opinion of their own.

Science has its explanation, and then within the scientific community, each scientist's understanding is slightly different.

The pastor who led that church service has his interpretation, my Dad has his, and I, the guy who experienced it all most intimately, have mine … which is different to yours … and which has evolved over the years so that it is not the same today as it was five years ago.

So, to me, that's not the point, because we could debate it for generations without ever reaching an equal understanding. We might even go to war over it and then start a business, dealing in arms.

The point is that it happened.

Whether we agree on a god, aliens, or little angels that run around inside our brains is all just fluff that deflects our attention from the truth.

It happened. And the reality of that is what I needed to deal with.

I don't know. At first, I'm on this cool spiritual adventure, following the call of this Voice inside of me. I sacrifice my attachment to the material world, take on the challenge, and I absolutely love it.

Then I get confused and caught up in the very way of life that I initially walked away from. Stupid. Muzungu.

Then I have this accident from hell that I should not have lived through. I mean, if I had kept my seatbelt on, I would have been bolognaise inside that vehicle. But instead, I live.

Barely.

And then I'm lost in Zimbabwe, in some kind of coma or something, and through a series of 'random' and inexplicable sequences, Dad finds me and I get to hospital and my life is saved.

But for what?

Because I am a retard who needs to live on happy pills or else I could end up murdering someone or walking in front of a bus without even knowing it.

And now, all of a sardine, I am 'the miracle child' who gets another shot at life ... I mean, really?!

If everything truly happens for a reason, then what's the point?

Why am I here?

Why didn't I die?

Jesus, I'm asking the same bloody questions that I was asking at the very beginning, and I feel as ignorant and lost as I did back then!

So this is the head-space I was in when I pitched tent,

when I withdrew from the world ... again,

when I went in search of answers that I only trusted I could find within my own self,

my own heart,

my own Soul.

Part of me wished that I had died on the side of the road in Makuti. That story made sense to me. But then there was a little part inside of me … a tiny spark somewhere in my deepest darkness that flickered with a crazy intensity of hopeful excitement, as if everything I was going through was all perfectly orchestrated and according to plan.

And I didn't know which part of me to trust, which part of me was true.

So that's why I went into my tent.

If there is one thing I know and am willing to bet my life on, it is that wisdom is found in silence. And that is what I craved more than life itself.

Silence.

Stillness.

To hear nothing, so that I could hear my Voice.

Somehow, I knew that if I could find silence, that I would find my next step. And so, not only did I remove myself from all the noise and clutter that our wonderfully advanced civilisation brings to us, but I also removed food from my life so that I could silence the craving voice of my body and allow my ears a better chance of hearing that still, small Voice of my Soul.

Day 1 was fun. I felt like a warrior about to enter the battlefield to conquer ancient enemies. I created a hero character in my mind, and transformed myself into him. Very boyish, I know, but I do weird things like that to motivate myself.

Day 2 and the battle began as my body started sending urgent messages to my brain, demanding food. At this stage, I could either succumb to my body's craving, or I could master my thoughts and return a message to my body that it was being greedy, paranoid and unreasonably fearful.

And that's what I chose to do, to establish my authority over my physical self, so that my spiritual self would awaken and find space to rise.

It was a day of severe hunger pains and anxiety, as my thoughts boiled in the vicious cauldron that was my mind, tormenting me from every side, giving me no space for a single peaceful breath.

At some stage though, I faded into sleep.

Day 3 and the battle continued, but a subtle change took place. I'm not sure how it worked, but my thoughts slowed down, like someone had reduced the heat under the cauldron so that the boiling pot settled into a gentle simmer. Make no mistake, I was still hungry, but the frantic voices of fear, scarcity and panic that had tormented me the day before were slower … less frantic … almost as if they didn't believe themselves as much as they had the day before. The result was that I was able to catch each thought as it appeared and deny it permission to re-enter my thinking. One by one, I picked them off, until I drifted into a sleep that held the promise of peace.

And then somewhere in Day 4, it felt like I slipped into an alternate reality. Very difficult to describe. Almost as if the barriers of the physical realm melted slightly and I found myself connected to the universe in some kind of energy field. It was a space of absolute stillness, exactly what I had been yearning for.

I took my guitar out my tent and wandered around the garden, singing to Nature until I emptied myself and silence overcame me.

I was finally prepared.

Day 5, and I awoke.

Zandspruit.

Like a single star gently coming into sight as the day loses its light, this word flickered within me. I knew the Voice all too well and had missed its song.

I was home.

A few days before I went into the tent, there was a church leaders meeting. My Dad invited me to tag along with him, and I decided to accept the invitation because there was promise of pizza. While the elders all chatted about things that didn't really interest me, and while I stuffed my face with pizza, I remember someone mentioning the word 'Zandspruit'.

At that time, I learned that Zandspruit was the name of an informal settlement, a *squatter camp*, just down the road from where my parents lived; a place I had never been aware of.

The reason it was mentioned at that church leaders meeting was because the church felt it on their hearts to get involved in the community in some way, as an act of outreach, but they didn't know how, or who would lead that. The topic was dropped, the meeting moved on, and I continued eating my pizza until it was time to go home.

Unlike Cafe Bardeli, nine years earlier, I didn't pay any attention to Zandspruit, and it did not remain in my thoughts. But on Day 5 in my tent, as soon as I heard the Voice bring Zandspruit into my consciousness, I knew that something was on. I went into my parent's house, picked up the phone and called my father.

"Dad, do we have any contacts in Zandspruit?" I began.

My father gave me the number for Paul-the-pastor. I called him and asked the same question, he gave me the number of a guy called Khubeka, who was another pastor that led a church in the settlement, and then I called him.

"Brother Khubeka." I started. "My name is Philén. You don't know me, but I got your number from pastor Paul." I continued. "Anyway, I have just been fasting and praying, and I believe that I have been called to Zandspruit. So I'm calling you."

It was a bit of a going-nowhere sentence, neither a solid statement nor a question, but I didn't know what else to say, because I didn't know what else was going on. Oddly enough, what I had to say was sufficient for the moment, because pastor Khubeka responded, with a noticeable tone of hopeful gratitude.

"My brother." he said. "I am at a conference in Port Elizabeth, and I have just been praying with a group of men, asking God to send more workers into Zandspruit. You are welcome."

I packed up my tent, walked out the house and towards the road, where I jumped onto a minibus taxi.

"*Uyaphi?*" (Where are you going?) The conductor questioned.

"Zandspruit." I responded, with certainty, as I stepped in to take my seat.

As the minibus moved forward, I looked around me, greeted the other passengers, and smiled inwardly. I felt like I was back in Zambia, catching a taxi from Chipata to Katete. It felt real. And as

I stared out the window, waiting to see what the inside of a squatter camp looked like, and why I was called to go there, I drifted into thought...

It's not over. I thought maybe it was, that maybe my Journey had come to an end, but it's not like that. Sure, I still feel far away from what I went in search of. I don't feel that I have the answers I want. In fact, if I'm honest with myself, I know less today than I did when I started.

But maybe that's it.

Maybe I'm not supposed to know.

Maybe it is in the unknowing that I remain alive.

Maybe it is the questions that drive the Journey, and without them I am dead.

Maybe the point is not to reach some place of absolute truth, but to always remain humble in the knowledge that I am just a fragment of a far greater work of art, and so my duty is to never stop asking, seeking and learning...

And I continued to let my mind wander, until I felt

the taxi slow down, and heard the voice of the conductor.

"Zandspruit."

The taxi stopped, the sliding door opened, and I stepped out. In front of me I saw a sprawling city of shanty-town-style shacks.

Waste pieces of metal, wood and board were used to make up these shacks that were packed tightly next to each other, as far as my eyes could see. There was barely enough space between them for people to walk.

The ground was pulverised into dust by thousands of travelling feet, and people were everywhere, talking, walking and laughing.

I didn't see any goats, but the chickens were around, as were the shebeens and spaza shops.

Men and boys were on bicycles, although there were a lot more vehicles than I grew used to in Zambia.

Children were running around, barefoot and free, as if they were in the village.

And the sweet rhythm and lyrics of the prophet,

Bob Marley, drifted through the air.

It all felt so familiar, yet with the skyline of Johannesburg city as the backdrop, it was all so different.

I stood my ground and soaked it all in.

As my thoughts unraveled, I saw the rastaman in his little shack-shop, selling vegetables and loose sweets to the children.

I walked over to him.

"Ahoy man." I started.

"Ahoy, my brother." Rasta responded.

And like a boy cannot resist the urge to follow the first firefly his eyes ever land on – desperately curious to discover where it goes – I just knew that I was exactly where I was supposed to be; that the Journey is the destination and there is no finish line.

All I could do was just keep walking ...

Twenty years from now you will be more disappointed by the things that you didn't do than by the ones you did do.

So throw off the bowlines.

Sail away from the safe harbour.

Catch the trade winds in your sails.

Explore. Dream. Discover.

- Mark Twain

13

The Final Word

I have found more questions than answers along the Way. I have discovered more fallibility in my thinking than I was initially prepared to accept. My mindset has shifted and my world view has evolved, but I have become aware of how much room still remains for me to grow.

I started my Journey in search of Love, Freedom and True Community. I definitely found Freedom and True Community – Ubuntu – but Love is something that slipped off my radar. Truthfully, with my youthful exuberance, Freedom confused me a bit and I made some decisions that I probably would not make again. This abuse of Freedom took away from my experience of True Community, and I think it widened the gap between me and Love.

This is something I am mindful of, as I continue this Journey … because it is not over … not by a long shot.

I believe in a world of pure harmony, where humankind lives lovingly with each other and the Earth; where all our differences are embraced and crafted into the most amazing symphony that echoes across the universe, carrying Life, Love and Healing wherever it flows.

I believe that an awakening has been taking place since we fell asleep. I don't know when that was, but I am convinced that it happened; that humanity was birthed with limitless potential, but that somewhere along the way, our thinking became corrupt and we lost belief in our God-given abilities, our own Divinity.

I believe that this awakening is currently approaching a tipping point, where there will be a mass shift in consciousness across the globe, as we all tap into our Inner Voice to live spirit-led lives, consciously connected to each other and Nature, with Love.

And yes, I believe in a God, a Super-Being, an Intelligence, Wisdom and Love that exists beyond space and time, and who is in control of all things. But I won't go into definitions of this God because I believe that trying to define the indefinable is exactly what divides us from each other, which is the exact opposite of the natural laws of the universe. All I will say is that I believe God is Love, and the idea that Love is *for* a certain group of people and *against* everyone else is a narrow-minded and extremely dangerous one.

I believe that every human being is beautiful and precious, that each of you is designed to love me, and that I am designed to love you … it's just that we have both forgotten who we truly are and are currently enslaved to another set of instructions that have been downloaded to our brains. I believe that it is the unquestioning mind that is most vulnerable.

The beliefs that I hold keep me rising each day. They are the reason I live. I can't think of anything better than to play my part in it all and to share in the celebrations along the way as our beautiful planet is redeemed from the oppression, division and destruction that currently thrives. I could be mad, only time will tell. But if I am, then so are you and the billions of others who have the deep and inexplicable yearning.

I don't know if I will reach all that I dream of. I

don't even know if the sun will rise tomorrow. But I have learned that should I wake, and the world is still alive, that I will reach the day's end if I just keep walking.

I don't know where the road goes, or how much of what I believe is truth and how much is foolish dreaming. But what I do know is this: if I can dream it, then I can be it. And if I believe it, I will achieve it.

So I have two choices: either I live today with all my energy aligned with my beliefs, and pursue the passions of my heart … OR … I call myself a dreamer and a fool, and I step back into convention to work a job for a pension and a retirement plan, accumulating as much insurance and security as I can along the way, only to leave it all behind when my body fades to dust.

Without any judgment on anyone else, I choose Option 1. Maybe we'll meet along the Way.

My life and this book is worth nothing, without every person who has been a part of it. And while I will fail to mention everyone – and I apologise for this – I must give appreciation to as many as I can remember.

And I'm not talking about the kind of appreciation I used to pay at the border.

So let me begin...

Mum, you knew me first. You loved me first, and I would choose you over and over again, if I had the choice to repeat life as many times as I could. I will never understand how you managed to think about everything I ever needed, and I am truly grateful for all of it. Thank you for nurturing my love of books and stories, for teaching me discipline and the value in pursuing excellence, for your carefully guarded curry recipes, which are the best in the world ... shit, thank you for everything and the love I have for my own veggie garden! I love you with all my heart.

Dad, you're my hero. If I can be half the father you have been, then my children will be extremely fortunate. Your tenacious spirit, courage, vision and love are qualities I will aspire to, all my days. Thank you for believing in me. Thank you for setting me free. Thank you for teaching me to dream. You're a legend and I love you!

Aaaaahhh, Tibor, how many times have you saved my worthless butt! I will never know how much of a burden you carried, as my older brother, but I do know that if it wasn't for you, I would not have been able to take the risks that I have. I love you, man, you're my favourite brother!

Kimberly, what can I say. 13 years and what a journey! Thank you for being my friend. Thank you for all your incredible support. Thank you for being the instrument to teach me some deeply important life lessons that I am still learning, and will probably only understand in a few years time. You are a truly beautiful human being that makes the world a brighter place. I am blessed with every moment that we have ever shared.

And now, in totally random order...

To every character in this book, there would be no story without you. I love and appreciate each of you immensely.

And to all those who are not in the print version of my story, please know that I am deeply grateful to each of you for being you, and for those short moments we have shared when our lives intersected.

Banda, I love you man. Every moment with you reminds me of how beautiful life can be. There is no one I know that would've had the courage to just jump on a bus and pitch up in Katete, unannounced. Without you, my story is empty.

Everyone needs a **Sean Tucker** in their life. Thanks for being a bro, thanks for kicking my ass when I needed it most and for pushing me through my toughest times of self-doubt. And thanks for your courage in writing your book (www. unlearning.co.za). Somewhere in your struggle, I found the permission I needed to be honest about mine. And that has been a priceless gift.

Craig Mclachlan, Craig Dennyson and **Grant Barnes-Webb**, you guys were the first to review the infantile work of this book, way back when I was just getting started and couldn't get past the first chapter. I just want you to know that I could never have reached here without the part that you played. Thank you.

Cheryl, you appeared from nowhere, at a time when I was most stagnant. I remain astounded by how many hours you devoted to this project and how much of my crap you endured through it all. You helped shape me from being an arrogant fool to a sincere storyteller. I owe you a huge debt of gratitude.

Jo and Debbie, you guys are my design heroes, I absolutely love the book cover! Thank you so much for how willingly you sacrificed your time and skills. Debbie, a special thank you goes out to you, for how quickly you jumped on to help, when I was completely without hope.

Aunty Margy, thank you for cruising through all 200+ pages of this book in just a couple of days, proofing it for me. Wow, you are a machine!

Bridget Simcox, you appeared when I was faltering at the finish line and needed a professional and fresh set of eyes to review my work before I could be confident to submit. Your input gave me the confidence I needed to finally release my work with peace. Thank you.

Sarah Morrow, when I was suffering through my greatest writer's block, and decided to try and find shortcuts to get around it by using a voice recorder, thank you for being available.

Kevan Mcnamara, thank you for jumping on stage at Swakop during one of those crazy New Year's Eve parties. "There is no finish line" is originally yours. Thank you for it. There was no better heading for my final chapter. And no you may not claim royalties.

The RCA church, you were praying for me before I really knew you. I don't know how it all works, but I cannot deny that something mysterious took place through it all, which guided my father to me in that Zimbabwean hospital, and saved my life. You have been an amazing family and I owe you a HUGE debt of gratitude. Thank you.

Brendon Keightley, God knows I needed someone like you to break through my stubborn heart. I love you, boetie. Thank you for playing your part in leading me to that crazy-ass church where I was miraculously healed.

Speaking of which, **Solid Rock Church**, I can't say much about much, but I do know that it was through your ministry that I received some significant healing. And I am sincerely grateful to you and the Christ, who you serve.

Sammy, Nat and Sir Keith, thank you for every coffee and tea moment that we've shared. I cannot tell you how important these have been to me in my own personal development and, without them, I surely would not have completed this work.

Sarah, Pete van O, Sarah-Louise, Sean and **Bonnie**, thank you so much for taking on the task of reviewing the first three chapters, at a time when I desperately needed a fresh set of eyes.

Sarah, you helped me to guard against romanticising another culture, just because it was an easy escape.

Peetrus, your encouragement from the start has been a huge support, thank you for helping me to not over-spiritualise my story.

Sarah-Louise, thank you for making me aware of the bitterness that I still held, regarding colonialism and the damage it did to Africa. You helped me to move past the blame game, and to take ownership of the here-and-now.

Bonnie, your feedback really got me thinking about how to build a stronger intro, and I am well-stoked with how it turned out.

Sean, your encouragement was so well timed, I don't think you will ever know how much I needed it!

I appreciate each of you immensely.

Sonja Kruse, The Ubuntu Girl (I seriously encourage you to Google this woman), you are a freaking legend. Thank you for being you, for walking your Path and confirming that I am not alone in this Journey and pursuit of an Ubuntu-driven Africa. Thanks also for being white and female, because that makes it so much more difficult to deny how Ubuntu is for everyone!

Phillipa Mitchell of Red Pepper Books, thank you for your generosity in sharing all the knowledge you have on how the world of book distribution works. Wow, I truly appreciate you.

Jolandie Rust (www.jorust.com), you are living proof that balls do not solely belong to men. You are an inspiration to women and children around the world, and we can all learn from your courage and persistence.

Brendon Naidoo, It is you who got me to consider that maybe … just maybe there was something that I was missing. This little gem of advice is what opened my Path again, when I thought the Journey had ended. I appreciate you, man.

Dan Eldon, author of The Journey is the Destination. Thank you for your life, your book, and that beautiful statement that summed up my story like no other words could have done.

And finally, to you, **the Reader**.

Thank you for your courage in your own Journey.

Thank you for asking the questions that you're asking.

And thank you for partnering with me in this incredible Journey of Life. Without you, I had no reason to push through those times when I felt like quitting.

May my story encourage you to share yours, and may yours be tons better than mine. And as we each continue to take ownership of our life's stories, may we slowly shed the shackles of our conditioning that has limited our potential for so many generations.

May we stand together, rise up, reclaim our identities, and establish our legacy here on

Earth, for the future generations to look upon with gratitude and Love.

I wish you an abundance of peace, and a belly-ache full of joy.

The spirit of holiness within me gives honour to the spirit of holiness within you. Namasté

FOLLOW THE JOURNEY

from Zandspruit to India and Beyond...

www.mylifemyafrica.org

6309297R00189

Printed in Great Britain
by Amazon.co.uk, Ltd.,
Marston Gate.